VISIONARY SPIRES

VISIONARY SPIRES

EDITED BY

Sarah Crewe

WITH CONTRIBUTIONS BY

Peter Williams
Jessica Harness
Alice Ryder

RIZZOLI
NEW YORK

597 Fifth Avenue, New York, NY 10017.

ISBN 0-8478-0660-X
LC 85-43038

Library of Congress
Cataloging-in-Publication Data
Main entry under title:
Visionary Spires.
1. Church architecture – Themes, motives.
2. Church architecture – Designs and plans.
1. Williams, Peter.
NA4810.V57 1986   726′.5   85-43038
ISBN 0-8478-0660-X

Designed by *Siobhan Keaney*.
Typeset by *Type Generation Ltd.*, London.
Printed and bound in Great Britain
by *Butler & Tanner Ltd.*,
Frome & London

Contents   *PAGE*

Introduction   7

Chapter 1
Pierced Air–the Spires of Northern Europe   14

Chapter 2
Towards St. Peter's Rome   20

Chapter 3
Milan Cathedral–'A work of such fame and importance'   38

Chapter 4
Baroque: The Dramatic Revolt   48

Chapter 5
Sir Christopher Wren and St. Paul's   57

Chapter 6
Restraint and Display in the Eighteenth Century   66

Chapter 7
The Return to Gothic   75

Chapter 8
The Cathedral Age in America   88

Chapter 9
'Simply Astounding'–St. John the Divine, New York   97

Chapter 10
Liverpool Cathedral–'a wholesome warning to architects'   104

Chapter 11
Sir Edwin Lutyens – The Last Great Endeavour   120

Chapter 12
Cologne and other Completions   128

Acknowledgments   139
Architectural Terms   140
Further Reading   141
Index   142

INTRODUCTION

'The view up Ludgate Hill is dominated by St. Paul's Cathedral, its façade flanked by small domed turrets, behind which rises Wren's slender spire. The spire, resting on a flat dome like an upturned saucer, rises to a secondary dome, then ascends, tier by tier, like an attenuated wedding-cake.' If this description does not represent the St. Paul's we know now, that is entirely as it should be. Yet it is a portrait of the design that received the Royal Warrant from King Charles II to proceed; the cathedral we now possess is a departure in nearly every aspect from the scheme that all involved with the cathedral might have expected to see built.

The many cathedrals that Sir Christopher Wren proposed for St. Paul's are discussed in a later chapter, but the Warrant Design illustrates the point that our greatest and most familiar cathedrals would have been very different had either their original designs been adhered to, or had the suggested alterations of later generations been executed. Architects' responses to the challenge of fulfilling the most demanding of briefs: to create a church whose majesty and beauty reflected its purpose as the noble house of God, have for centuries been amongst the greatest works of man, but have often never got beyond exquisite designs on paper.

The reasons are various. Sometimes a church left unfinished attracted the attention of those who wished to complete it, but lack of funds, violent disagreement amongst patrons or more sadly, inertia, precluded the use of designs advocated by the architects.

1 Sir Christopher Wren's Warrant Design for St. Paul's Cathedral, with its bizarre spire.

2 Nicholas Hawksmoor's alarming, domed Westminster Abbey that fortunately remained unbuilt.

In some cases this was fortunate. Westminster Abbey, coronation church of the English royal family, languished without western towers till the eighteenth century, when Nicholas Hawksmoor supplied the towers that now complement the medieval church. He had however proposed more sweeping alterations: the Muniments Room at the Abbey possesses his drawing showing the church dominated by a low dome on a heavy square base, a dome fenced in by squat Gothic turrets. The transepts below it were to be given a Gothic veneer but with classical features added, while the nave would have had simple Gothic buttresses and windows. In order to execute this scheme it would have been necessary to demolish the crossing of the medieval church, destroy the rose windows, sculpture, and all original work in the transepts, as well as plane off all the thirteenth- and fifteenth-century work on the nave. The bulk of the medieval abbey would have vanished.

PLATE I

James Wyatt, nicknamed 'The Destroyer' for his aggressive restoration work on numerous cathedrals, including Salisbury, intended a spire with delicate flying buttresses for the central tower of Durham Cathedral. His drawing dated 1795 depicts this intended 'Lanthorn and Spire' for a cathedral which originally bore two western spires. Wyatt's larger ideas for Durham (including – horrifyingly – a plan to demolish the western Galilee Chapel to make way for a dramatic coachway to the cathedral for the bishop) were stillborn; but the central spire would have given an elegant focus to the long, low building.

3 James Wyatt's delicate drawing, dated 1795, of the spire he advocated for Durham cathedral.

4 Durham Cathedral today, without a central spire.

5 Chester Cathedral in the mid-nineteenth century, its soft sandstone severely eroded.

6 The spire that George Gilbert Scott suggested for Chester, published in 1868.

Chester Cathedral would have benefited in a similar way had all Scott's restoration work reached fruition. Prior to his involvement, the red sandstone cathedral had mouldered away, all external ornament eroded. Scott had to reface the church completely but the major addition of an elegant lead and wood spire to top the low central tower, proposed in 1868, was never adopted.

More impressive, more majestic and sadly more frequently doomed to failure were the myriad designs for entirely new cathedrals. This book celebrates the greatest of them: St. John the Divine, New York; Lille, Truro, Edinburgh Cathedrals, and perhaps most prodigious of all, Liverpool Cathedral. While the many submissions for this church are discussed in the chapter on Liverpool, a further example is given here to show not only the scale of proposed churches, but the beguiling, persuasive way that these were sometimes presented in their urban setting. James Brooks's cathedral of 1886 is an early French Gothic one, made more splendid by the perspective view from the south-east published in *The Builder*. It shows the cathedral not in terms of a dry technical drawing, but as a dramatic element in a city skyline.

7 A persuasive vision for Liverpool by James Brooks, showing the cathedral in its setting.

"Deserted"

"MY TABERNACLE IS SPOILED, AND ALL MY CORDS ARE BROKEN. MY CHILDREN ARE GONE FORTH OF ME, AND THEY ARE NOT"

8 H. W. Brewer's fantasy 'Deserted' depicted a city over which soared the House of God.

The lure for architects and artists of the idea of a visionary cathedral was perhaps most evocatively depicted by the English draughtsman H. W. Brewer, who published finely worked views of extant churches and wistful views of an imagined past, of medieval cities over which rose massive churches. One of his views conveys the delicacy of his artistry: *'Deserted'*, with a northern European spire vaguely inspired by Antwerp, is a vision of an architectural fantasist, enthralled by the medieval period. The chance to design a cathedral, or major church, was the spur to achieve the highest levels of artistic excellence, although so often without hope of execution.

9 A design for a vast, centrally planned cathedral, that has been attributed to Inigo Jones and John Webb, now at Worcester College, Oxford.

A final example, a vast centrally planned cathedral, exists on paper from the seventeenth century. With an enormous dome, curving walls and a huge portico, it shows an awareness of church planning as developed in the Renaissance, and has been considered an influence on Wren's later work at St. Paul's. Yet it cannot accurately be attributed to a specific architect. John Webb and Inigo Jones are the most likely candidates; neither designed an executed cathedral; either would be a household name had it been built, in London or elsewhere. It, like so many other designs in this book, shows just how brilliant are the cathedrals and churches that we have been denied.

1. PIERCED AIR – THE SPIRES OF NORTHERN EUROPE

*T*hroughout the Middle Ages, architects worked to create an impressive church. The west fronts of cathedrals and abbeys across Europe were to be the gateways to God's House on Earth. As such they had to have a pair of western towers flanking the great portal. This twin-towered type of west front, so frequently used in Normandy in the Romanesque period, and indeed across Europe throughout the Gothic period, began to be slightly superseded as the Middle Ages reached their maturity. Instead of creating the symmetry of two towers rising at the west end of a major church, architects began to explore the possibility of one enormous tower, whether placed asymmetrically at the west front, or attached to the body of the church to the east.

Transition from the symmetrical type of west front, as typified by Rheims and Amiens, in France, and York, Lincoln, and Wells in England, can be seen at Strasbourg. Strasbourg had built a large, typically French west front in the mid-Gothic period, rising magnificently through three storeys. Then a preference for a different sort of façade manifested itself. The architect Michael Parler conceived of a single, vast west tower rising on a block of masonry placed between the western towers. This converted the first three storeys of the façade into a solid rectangle which would act as the base for a large towering openwork spire rising above it. His design of around 1385 is still preserved in the Musée de L'Oeuvre de Notre Dame. This scheme was certainly daring, but lacked elegance and was abandoned.

Between 1399 and 1419 another architect, Ulrich von Ensingen, erected a fourth stage on the north tower. This was an extraordinary combination of openwork carving and spiral staircases, an octagon contained by four large spiral staircase turrets. It was a work of great mathematical skill and audacity. This particular architect did not however go on to complete the north spire. This fell to his successor, Johan Hültz, who produced several designs – all of which relied on the use of open stonework and on creating a vast filigreed spire through which the wind could whistle. One of his designs is typically German, made up of ascending panels of geometrical ornament contained by square surrounds, quite similar to the spire at Freiburg Cathedral. But the spire as built was much more complex. It is a bizarre arrangement of pinnacles and staircases, so encrusted with ornament as almost to lose the octagonal ground plan. As a result of this work, completed in 1439, the master builders of the Holy Roman Empire conferred the title of Grand-Master on the Master of the Lodge of Strasbourg, while the city itself became the Grand Chapter of the Order: both honours were granted in perpetuity. At 466 feet high, this is the largest stone spire ever to be built in the Middle Ages and understandably, increased the general desire for vast vertical structures.

An equally impressive tower was built in Vienna. Vienna Cathedral, dedicated to St. Stephen, did not have a typical Gothic west front, instead its towers were planned to rise in transeptal positions, that is north and south of the body of the church. The southern tower was completed between 1368 and 1433, and is again a triumph of the Germanic enthusiasm for highly decorated pierced stonework, rising to a height of 448 feet. Even more audacious was the tower for the church at Ulm. The vast church was conceived in 1377 and the foundation stones laid. The west tower was inspired by Ulrich von Ensingen who, as we know, was responsible for the great work at Strasbourg; both churches share the use of the inter-penetration of space, of stone and air mixed in a vertiginous, light yet substantial way. Ulrich von Ensingen's original design was built to its third storey late in the fifteenth century under the architect Matthaus Boblinger. He proposed an even more elaborate spire on an octagonal base, but when building began, it was found that he had not remembered to strengthen the foundations. When signs of collapse were visible by 1493, the architect was dismissed for incompetence and a conference of twenty master masons was called to discuss what should happen next. One of these, Burkhard Engelberg, moved into the controlling position, and managed successfully to stabilise the structure of the tower, as well as continuing the building of the body of the church. At the advent of the sixteenth century, Ulm, like many other German cities, began to feel the impact of the Reformation. During the religious wars of the 1520s, the church was stormed, and vast numbers of works of art destroyed, including the enormous and costly high altar. It was not an auspicious time at which to be continuing the west tower, and work came to a halt, to be resumed according to Boblinger's original design in the nineteenth century. His slender, opulent octagonal spire now rises to 528 feet, making it easily the largest stone tower designed in the Middle Ages actually to be erected. What is notable about Ulm is that the church was never a cathedral; instead it was the result of the city's determination to have one of the greatest churches ever built, for as Ulm became the figurehead of the Swabian League in the fourteenth century, it was desirable to have a church that reflected its new importance. It is today merely a Lutheran parish church, but one crowned, perhaps more than any other parish church, by a spire and tower that overwhelms its city and nearby surroundings.

These spires were very much the emblems and landmarks of their cities, and indeed their very grandeur could sometimes put them at risk. That at Strasbourg, for example, was considered in the French Revolution, a period in which all ecclesiastical art forms were in danger of destruction, to offend principles of equality; the egalitarian régime in the city found it provocative and its destruction was only circumvented when a quick-thinking admirer of the church managed to put a vast liberty cap on top of the spire, making it subservient to revolutionary ideals, but ensuring its survival.

Strasbourg, Ulm, Vienna; three examples where vast openwork spires of the later Middle Ages were actually built. Northern Europe can furnish several more monumental schemes which exist only on paper or parchment. The Belgian church of Malines, sometimes called Mechlin, is a splendid instance. In 1452 Andries Keldermans began a huge single west tower of the cathedral which was continued by his son Antoon; this family was one of the most important Netherlandish architectural clans, and contributed much to the fifteenth-century appearance of that part of Europe. Malines's tower was to have been a vast undertaking, for which the original design still exists. Indeed, material was actually carved and gathered together for its upper storey. This material, which would have added another 300 feet to the already large western tower, was piled up near the cathedral, but in Belgium, as in Germany, the sixteenth century was not a period when religious endeavours were given a completely uninterrupted run. In 1578 the carved masonry was commandeered for war purposes, to be used ignominiously for the construction of the fortress of Willemstad in 1583. Fortunately Hollar engraved the design for the cathedral's tower and in the nineteenth century the enthusiastic English architectural draughtsman, H.W. Brewer, created a romantic scene of the cathedral completed according to its medieval intentions.

At the church of Ste. Waudru, Mons, an even taller structure was intended, and a drawing survives for a west spire 600 feet high. The structure was begun in 1535 as the great termination of an immense collegiate church. The tower was intended to be nearly 200 feet higher than the existing spire of Antwerp Cathedral, and would have been the largest stone structure built in the Middle Ages. Unfortunately it, like so many other churches of the time, proved impossible to execute. Fortuitously its design was published in 1844 by M.R. Chalon, and copies are still extant. There is an example of it in the Victoria and Albert Museum, London, which has been recently conserved. Had this been built it would have been genuinely one of the wonders of the later Middle Ages.

The west front conceived for Louvain can make claims as grand as Ste. Waudru; it would have been less tall, but as grand. For this the original drawing and a model still survive in the Town Hall. It was designed in 1507, conceived for the collegiate church of St. Pierre. The intention was to have a tower at the west end, 535 feet high, flanked by two others of a mere 435 feet. It was started by the architect Metsis following the model mentioned. The problem here was that the foundations were laid rather stupidly on shifting sands, and almost immediately the towers began to show signs of cracking and disintegration. All too soon the very incomplete towers had to be truncated to a fifth of their intended size, leaving Louvain with the lower storeys of one of the most imaginative architectural concepts of the sixteenth century.

These northern towers show architects intending to outdo each other and indeed outdo gravity in their determination to create something quite majestic, quite vertiginous. That any have been built at all must be a cause for celebration; that so many were condemned to being merely churches on paper is a cause for regret.

10 Wenceslaus Hollar's engraving of Strasbourg Cathedral of *c.*1656.

11 The ground plan of the spire at Strasbourg Cathedral, now in the Victoria and Albert Museum, London.

12 Johan Hültz's spire for Strasbourg was more controlled than that which was eventually built.

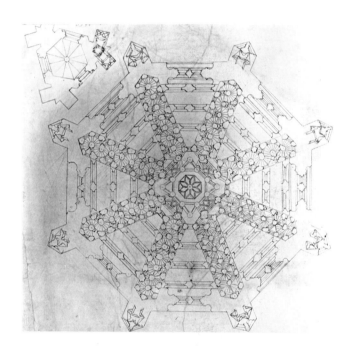

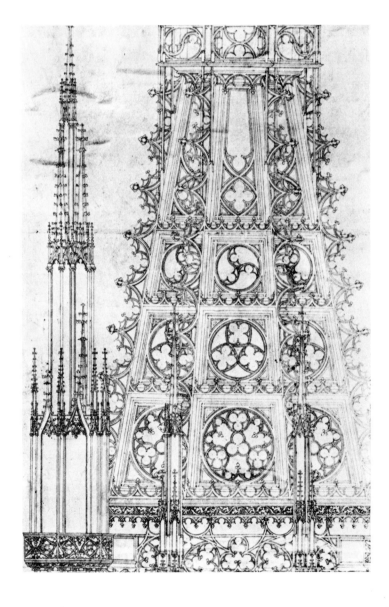

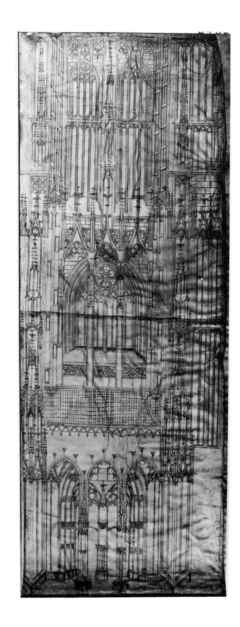

13 A medieval design for the lower storeys of
    Ulm Minster, now in the Victoria and
    Albert Museum, London.

14 Ste. Waudru, Mons. Typical of several late
    Gothic towers in northern Europe that were
    never completed, it exhibits the flamboyant
    tracery and Curvilinear gables that were
    prevalent at the time.

15 Malines Cathedral, Belgium, lost the carved stonework for its spire to the sixteenth-century Wars of Religion, when the assembled masonry was removed to build a fortress. The design was engraved by Hollar, and H. W. Brewer reconstructed the cathedral as it was originally intended, for the fantasy published in *The Builder*.

2. TOWARDS ST. PETER'S ROME

St. Peter's, Rome, is a powerful symbol; it is the centre of the Catholic Church and the crowning achievement of the Renaissance. While it was being built it had a central role in art, politics and religion, and one which was influential throughout Europe. Contributing to its status and particularly to our understanding of the period is the series of magnificent unbuilt cathedrals which lie behind Carlo Maderno's seventeenth-century façade or in the archives of the Vatican.

For a post-medieval cathedral, the building of St. Peter's took a long time: over 200 years passed between Rossellino's first project and Bernini's completed Piazza. Fortunately we can observe its progress through a wealth of plans, models and engravings by many of the major artists of the day including Raphael and Michelangelo. The period saw rapid political and religious changes: the Protestant Revolt and the Catholic Reformation, the Sack of Rome and a series of ambitious popes. In artistic terms, St. Peter's is the one building that could be said to represent Renaissance, Mannerist and Baroque ideals and, as has been proven, there is more than enough material for a whole book on the subject. The aim of this chapter is to celebrate the best of the designs and catch some of the atmosphere surrounding this giant commission.

Nicholas V was the pope who instigated the rebuilding of the old Constantinian basilica of St. Peter's, but his attempts to 'testify to the handiwork of Our Lord' through the grandeur and endurance of a great church was unsuccessful. He had called the Tuscan, Bernardo Rossellino to Rome in 1447 but the architect's submission of a Latin cross design only got as far as the choir behind the apse of the old basilica. According to Manetti, the aim of this plan was to build the new St. Peter's in the form of the human body, with the transept representing the open arms and the tribune the head, so that it symbolised, through contemporary philosophy, the cosmos and the universe. Whilst this aim was never fulfilled by Rossellino's plan, such symbolism persisted, but in changing forms. Gianlorenzo Bernini's colonnade was likened in the seventeenth century to the open arms of St. Peter guiding the Christian to the centre of his faith, a dramatic rather than symbolic interpretation of the image, typical of the difference between the Renaissance beginning of St. Peter's and its Baroque conclusion.

The details of the next phase of building (1505-14) are unclear, but it was undoubtedly prompted by the desires of Pope Julius II, who was elected on 1st November 1503. He launched himself with extraordinary fervour into a scheme for the rebuilding of Rome to rival Imperial Rome and to represent the highest artistic achievements of the Renaissance, in competition with the cultural centres of Tuscany. It was he who decided some time before the summer of 1505, probably in consultation with Donato Bramante, that the old and crumbling St. Peter's would have to be pulled down, after 1200 years of uninterrupted worship, in order to make room for a building of sufficient scale to symbolise the power and glory of this new Rome, and to house Julius II's own tomb. Michelangelo had received the commission for the mausoleum in 1505, and had designed a free-standing tomb of enormous scale; thus the problem of finding it an architectural setting became crucial. Michelangelo had suggested putting the tomb in Rossellino's choir, but others such as the Pope's architectural adviser, Giuliano da Sangallo, counselled the Pope that a chapel on a centralised plan should be built specially to house it. Three parts of St. Peter's had therefore to be co-ordinated, a centrally planned chapel or church to house Julius II's tomb, the existing tomb of the Apostle of St. Peter, housed in the old basilica and around which the whole of the religious function of the cathedral was based, and Rossellino's unfinished choir. These were the terms of the debate that was to produce so many designs of quality.

Donato Bramante (who was already working on the reorganisation of the Vatican Palace), Giuliano da Sangallo, both Tuscans, and Fra Giocondo (who had been specially summoned from Paris because of his technical expertise) all submitted plans, whose order and exact authorship is often unclear. The chronology is probably complicated by the fact that the Pope was consulting so many architects, and unrecorded mutual decisions may well have been made in between the various plans and their execution. What is clear is that a centralised plan by Bramante was accepted, since it is recorded in a medal by Caradosso, cast in 1506 and buried under the foundation stone of St. Peter's on

18th April. This medal shows one characteristic – a large, centrally placed dome – which was to survive all subsequent changes.

According to Vasari's life of Bramante, this plan was 'the result of an infinite number of drawings', some of which we shall be looking at in more detail later. It is a Greek cross, a plan that had been frequently used in Byzantine architecture of the ninth century, thus a fitting historical reference to the early origins of St. Peter's. It has four apses so identical that it is not possible to tell which was to hold the high altar; the main dome was to be surrounded by minor domes over corner chapels and by towers in the corners further out still. Given the powerful tradition of longitudinal planning, it is fascinating that this plan should have been accepted for this most important of western churches over more conventional basilical plans, such as that submitted by Fra Giocondo. There was no precedent at all for the working out of such a plan on the kind of scale conceived by Bramante.

Our curiosity is aroused by Bramante's only partly executed scheme. How did Bramante come to such an unusual and symbolically perfect artistic conclusion? What does it tell us about the history of St. Peter's or Renaissance humanism as a whole?

Bramante had grown up in Urbino, where Piero della Francesca painted; Sabba Castiglione described him as 'a cosmographer, a poet in the Italian language, and valiant painter, as a disciple of Mantegna and a great perspectivist as a pupil of Piero della Francesca, and so excellent in architecture . . .'. Perhaps more importantly, Urbino was also where Francesco di Giorgio wrote his treatise on architecture, which included a discussion of central planning. In the 1480s and 1490s Bramante worked for Lodovico Sforza in Milan, where it seems likely that he saw Antonio Filarete's *Tratto di Architettura* (1461-64) and its eccentric visions of domed churches for the Sforzinda. In Milan he also worked in 1488 on Sta. Maria delle Grazie, where aesthetic and functional considerations led him to adopt an embryonic central plan for the extension of the medieval church. Surely, too, he must have exchanged views with Leonardo and Francesco di Giorgio when the three men met to discuss work on Milan's cathedral in 1490. It cannot be mere coincidence that Leonardo's sketchbooks reveal not only the famous diagrams of man's body as a mathematical and religious symbol which fit Manetti's description of Rossellino's St. Peter's, but also several sketches of domed centralised churches emerging, like Bramante's plan, almost organically from a cluster of peripheral chapels.

The next step we may chart towards St. Peter's must be Bramante's Tempietto of S. Pietro in Montorio, Rome, of 1502. Looking at the two buildings one could be forgiven for thinking that the Tempietto was an architectural trial piece for St. Peter's. The clear aesthetic balance and round colonnaded form of the monument drew stylistically on the round temples of classical Rome, yet the monument's function was religious, it marked the spot on which St. Peter was supposed to have been crucified. This fusion of classical style and contemporary religious function was an absorbing task for the Renaissance intellectual. Julius II's political aim was to restore central authority by similar reference to Imperial Rome and to Rome as the centre of the Christian world. The actual political power of Rome was vested in Spain at this time and so cultural achievements were even more important to propagate the myth of Roman renewal.

The Tempietto was conceived as a totally centralised expression, a complete, pure form dominating the space around it, sadly something now lost to the building. In Bramante's plan St. Peter's would have commanded the space on all sides too, without the directional emphasis given by the later additions. The simplicity of the proportions gives the Tempietto classical dignity and its unadorned Tuscan Doric order forbidding grandeur, in a way that Bramante perfected in his designs for St. Peter's. Despite the difference in scale, it seems a simple step from the Tempietto to the cathedral. The treatise of Francesco di Giorgio had related centrally planned structures to religious symbolism and seen the dome as an image of the vault of the heavens, but the following passage from Marsilio Ficino in his commentary on Plato's *Symposium* gives the fullest idea of the symbolic significance of the new forms and the kind of theories that were current in the intellectual circle to which Bramante and some of his colleagues working on St. Peter's belonged:

And it was not without reason, that the ancient theologians placed Goodness at the centre: and in the circle Beauty. I say surely Goodness in a centre: and in four circles Beauty. The only centre of all things is God. The four circles which continually revolve around God are the Mind, the Soul, Nature and Matter. The Angelic Mind is a fixed circle: the Soul, in itself mobile: Nature moves in others, but not through others; Matter, not only in others, but also by others is moved. But why do we call God the Centre and those other four circles? Shall we declare? The Centre is the point of the circle which is fixed and indivisible: from where many lines divisible and mobile lead to their similar circumference. This circumference, which is divisible, revolves around the centre not otherwise than a round body revolves round a pivot. And such is the nature of the centre that, although it is one, indivisible and fixed, nevertheless it is found in each part of many, if not all, of the mobile and divisible lines: since in each part of each line is the point. But the reason why no thing can be unlike its own is as follows. The lines leading from the circumference towards the centre cannot touch this point except by a point of their own which is equally simple, unique and immobile. Who will deny that God is rightly called the centre of all things? Considering that in all things He is unique, simple and immobile: and that all things which are produced by Him are multiple, compound and in a sense mobile: and just as they go away from him, so too in the way of lines or circumferences they return to Him. In this way, the Mind, the Soul, Nature and Matter, which proceed from God strive to return to Him and from all sides with every diligence they revolve around Him. And just as the centre is found in each part of the line, and in the whole circle: and all lines by their point touch the point which is the centre of the circle, similarly God who is the centre of all things, who is most simple unity and most pure Act, places Himself in all things. Not only for the reason that He is present in all things, but also because He has given to all things created by Him some intrinsic share and very simple and active power which is called the unity of things: from which and to which, as from a centre to a centre of His, all other powers and parts depend on each part. And certainly it is necessary that all created things, rather than gathering round their own centre and their own unity, should come close to their Creator: so that through their own centre they should come close to the centre of all things.

This could almost be a description of the Tempietto and must be relevant to the persistence of domed structures from Florence to St. Peter's, in all its plans, and to the adoption of a domed structure by Sir Christopher Wren at St. Paul's, London.

Let us leave theory for a while and look at the practical function of the cathedral. Like the Tempietto and the old basilica, it was a *Martyrium* since it was to be erected over the tomb of the Apostle, and, since it was to house the Michelangelo tomb and the huge crowds which would be present at major church ceremonies, it was going to have to be very large. Of course the idea of a domed cathedral was not unprecedented. It is likely that Julius wished to rival the Duomo in Florence, with its dome by Brunelleschi and it is interesting that he called upon Tuscan artists to be involved in the building of St. Peter's and the aggrandisement of the Vatican apartments. Perhaps he also wished to rival that other great domed building of Western civilisation, Sta. Sophia in Constantinople, which was currently under Muslim control? Some of the reconstructions have a distinctly Islamic feel in their rising, domed shapes.

Given all these secondary meanings which Bramante, and presumably the other architects working on St. Peter's too, felt the need to build into the new St. Peter's, it is hardly surprising that little time was given the practical problems of restoring the old basilica and that so many plans should have been submitted before a final solution could be reached. Giuliano da Sangallo was in competition with Bramante from the start of the 1505 building programme and Otto von Förster argues convincingly from the dating of Sangallo's drawings that the Pope must have laid down a precise brief for his architects. This must have included requirements for a square plan with an inscribed cross, a central hemispherical dome surrounded by a number of minor chapels, and the whole in isolation from surrounding buildings. This casts a different light on the creation of the cathedral, dulling slightly the genius of Bramante.

Giuliano's plan in the Albertina, Vienna has a special simple beauty, and its solid walls would have firmly supported the vast dome. But, unlike Bramante's plans, it is an essentially unrelated fusion of the two shapes of neo-platonic theory, the square and the circle, and it was in response to this that Bramante finally produced his complex integrated design, the Parchment Plan. This plan is of beautifully rationalised spatial units combined with multiplicity, based on the complicated form of the irregular octagon. Yet the Parchment Plan was full of symbolism too. Three openings on each of the four façades corresponded to the celestial city of Jerusalem, and the four bell-towers symbolised the tribes of Judah, Ephraim, Daniel and Reuben, who presided over the tabernacle. The exterior, whilst corresponding closely to the architecture of the interior, had no plastic ornament and thus referred to the simplicity of the classical buildings known in their ruined form in Rome. It was as if, as is suggested by Portoghesi, Bramante and Giuliano were figureheads in the current debate: the former quoted from the classical world in terms of a coherent synthesised vision of all that be believed to be classical and was entrenched in ideology, while the latter quoted more directly from the antique. Much to the chagrin of the architect, the Parchment Plan was rejected on the grounds that it could not contain the tomb of the apostle. Had it been executed, it would have been both geometrically harmonious and yet quite climactic in its progression of forms. It would have been quite unlike anything ever built.

It was left to Bramante's followers to resolve the problem of matching his ideological perfection with the practical requirements of the cathedral. In this Peruzzi may have been one of the most influential followers, on the grounds that his plan from the Third Book of Serlio is so close to Bramante's that it is possible he was involved in his master's final plan. There are many drawings in the Uffizi, Florence, some more fantastical than others, which could be attributed to Peruzzi yet we only really know for sure that he was appointed assistant to Sangallo by Pope Paul II after the death of Raphael. Raphael assumed responsibility for the building in 1514, although his involvement was probably not very great. His plan is a simple resolution of Bramante's beginnings; he and Fra Giocondo had returned to a rather conventional Latin cross design. Perhaps the needs of the Counter-Reformation, the reassertion of Catholic doctrine, demanded expression in more conventional Gothic form in this dogmatic period, when Cardinal Carlo Borromeo was laying down the artistic rules for the Catholic countries. Whatever the reasons, it appears that Raphael took his responsibilities very seriously. He writes to Castiglione in 1514 of the 'great weight of the task of planning St. Peter's'. Vasari is not to be totally trusted in his opinions on Raphael, since Raphael was an ally of Bramante's, whereas Vasari's hero was Michelangelo, but he does imply in his life of Michelangelo that Raphael was more concerned with his own glorification than with the furtherance of St. Peter's. Perhaps we should take a fairly critical attitude of his comment in the same letter to Castiglione: 'But in my thoughts I fly much higher, I should like to find the beautiful forms of ancient buildings, though I know not if the flight will be like that of Icarus. A great light on them is held out to me by Vitruvius, but I do not know if it will suffice.' Perhaps Vasari was right in alerting us to the possibility that Raphael's concern for greater ornamentation on St. Peter's was not just a consequence of his developments in painting, which was becoming more and more decorative, but a self-seeking move to get the papacy to invest more money in St. Peter's. He says in a letter written to Pope Leo X with Castiglione, the following: 'The modern buildings are well known both for being new and for not having entirely attained either the excellence or that immense expense which one can see and observe in the old. For though in our days architecture is very alive and has come very close to the manner of the ancients, as is seen in many of the works of Bramante, nevertheless the ornamentation is not of such precious material as in the old . . . .'.

Michelangelo later chose not to be paid for his work on St. Peter's, and whilst it is consistent with what we know of his character that he should have stated this simply as a matter of pride, it is also possible that the architects working on St. Peter's were corrupt.

The next great contributor to St. Peter's was Antonio da Sangallo and in many ways his is the most beautiful scheme of all. Happily his plans can be seen in a large wooden model by Labacco now in the Museo Petriano, and one cannot help but see a relationship between this model and Wren's Great Model of St. Paul's; the campanili bear more relation to this than they do to the finished St. Peter's. Sangallo made no enormous changes to Bramante's design, he returned to the Greek cross plan and added raised ambulatories but aimed to keep the interior and exterior related as they had been in Bramante's design. Michelangelo's views on this design must be cited here, since they seem to have biased future generations against a plan which, though cumbersome as a model, had many fine elements. It shows loyalty to Bramante's conceptions combining his campanili (themselves a medieval symbol of wealth) with the dome, and adding a vestibule to a Greek cross in the way that Bramante had indicated as a possibility. Unfortunately Sangallo seems to have grasped the detail, which looks attractive in an engraving, but has not the necessary control for a building of Cyclopean scale. It took a giant of Michelangelo's status to resolve this problem. Just as Raphael had wanted greater ornamentation, Michelangelo dictated massive scale to control the disparate elements. We must view these plans not as competitors so much as indicators of the changing taste of the age. Michelangelo's criticism of Sangallo's work in Vasari's *Lives* provides the foundation for discussion of Michelangelo's own contribution:

"And it cannot be denied," Michelangelo wrote to Bartolomeo Ferratino in 1555, "that Bramante was as excellent an architect as anyone who has existed from ancient times onwards. He prepared the first plan for St. Peter's, not full of confusion but clear and distinct, luminous and isolated all around, so that it did not interfere with any part of the palazzo; and it was conceded a beautiful thing, as can still be seen; so that whoever has departed from the design of Bramante, as Sangallo has done, has departed from the truth; and that this is the case anyone with unimpassioned eyes can see in his model. By that circle which he makes outside it, he firstly takes away all light from the building of Bramante, and not only this, but in itself it has not any light at all; and there are so many dark hiding places between the top and bottom that they provide great opportunity for countless crimes such as: hiding outlaws, making false coins, imprisoning nuns, and other crimes, so that in the evening when the church was closed, twenty-five men would be needed to seek out those who remained hidden inside it, and they would have a hard task to find them. Then there would be this other difficulty, that by encircling Bramante's building with the projection shown in the model, it would be necessary to level to the ground the chapel of Paolo, the rooms of Piombo, the Ruota, and many others: not even the Sistine Chapel would, I think, remain untouched. Concerning the part made from the outside circle, which they say cost a hundred thousand crowns, this is not true, since it could be made for sixteen thousand, and by destroying it little would be lost, because the stones used there and the foundations could not become available at a more appropriate time, and the building would be improved by two hundred thousand crowns and three hundred years of time. This is how it seems to me and without passion; since to win would be a very great loss to me. And if you can make this clear to the Pope, you will do me pleasure, for I do not feel at ease.

In Michelangelo's work on St. Peter's we have the truest example of the artist believing he is working for God; he devoted seventeen years to the project until his death in 1564, and throughout that period did not receive direct payment. Michelangelo had come into contact with the followers of Erasmus, and had been one who hoped for reconciliation with the Protestants. This having failed, he threw himself into an introverted, tempestuous kind of mysticism and his work became a symbol of a true kind of Catholic reform, of belief in the essential strength of the Catholic Church as opposed to the shallow moralising which was affecting painting at the time. He exalted the power and prestige of Rome through his giant visions for St. Peter's, and instead of trying to express complex philosophy, as Bramante had in his Parchment Plan, he made his statement loud and clear.

The Council of Trent met for the first time in 1545, but interestingly did not lay down any rules against the central plan, only against round churches; St. Carlo Borromeo, the great writer of Counter-Reformation philosophy said that: a church should, in accordance with tradition, be of *cross plan;* round plans were used for the temples of pagan idols and seldom for Christian churches. In 1546-47 Michelangelo prepared a new model, which was faithfully adhered to, and presented his solution as a return to Bramante. In fact his design went further than Sangallo in eliminating the relationship between the interior and the exterior, a feature essential to Renaissance thought. He removed the 'projections' that he had disliked in Sangallo's model, but retained a continuous wall around the building of a single giant order quite unrelated to the inside. This pulled the church together, its scale giving unity to its disparate parts. He removed Sangallo's loggia and campanili, leaving the whole isolated as a Greek cross with a medieval façade. All its problems were bequeathed to the next generation. His perimeter wall, as we have seen in the quote from Vasari, reduced the cost of the whole building, and brought back the emphasis to the dome, which rises imperiously from the surrounding flowing shapes, and is defined with ribs like Brunelleschi's dome in Florence. Thanks to Vasari, this design received quite an unbalanced amount of praise:

> The Pope eventually gave his approval to the model Michelangelo had made. This diminished the size of St. Peter's but increased its grandeur in a manner which pleases all those able to judge, although there are some who claim to be experts (without justification) and who do not approve. Michelangelo found that four principal piers, made by Bramante and retained by Antonio da Sangallo, which were to help support the weight of the cupola, were weak; so he partly filled them in, making on each side two spiral stairways up which the beasts of

burden can climb with the materials, as can men on horseback, to the uppermost level of the arches.

> He made the first cornice above the travertine arches; this curves round gracefully and is a marvellous and distinctive piece of work, better than anything else of its kind. He also began the two great hemicycles of the crossing, and whereas previously, under the direction of Bramante, Baldassare Peruzzi and Raphael, as was said, eight tabernacles were being built on the side of the church facing the Campo Santo (and the same plan was followed by Sangallo) Michelangelo reduced the number to three, with three chapels behind them.

Etiènne Dupérac and Vasari were partly responsible for the concept of Michelangelo as 'Il Divino' and the inviolability of his plans is shown by Vasari's report that in 1565 Piero Ligorio was dismissed from the fabric of St. Peter's for trying to change Michelangelo's designs. The second passage from Vasari gives an idea of Michelangelo's power over popes and architects alike.

> Vasari had scarcely returned to Rome, just before the beginning of 1551, when the Sangallo clique, in a plot against Michelangelo, persuaded the Pope to summon to a meeting in St. Peter's all the builders and overseers, hoping to convince His Holiness by slanderous accusations that Michelangelo had ruined the building. Now Michelangelo had built ready for vaulting the hemicycle of the king of France (where the three chapels are) with the three upper windows; but now knowing what was to be done with the vault, and relying on their own poor judgement, they had convinced the elder Cardinal Salviati and Marcello Cervini (who later became Pope) that St. Peter's would be left poorly lit. So after they had all assembled the Pope told Michelangelo that the deputies alleged that the hemicycle would have little light.
> Michelangelo said: "I would like them to speak for themselves."
> Cardinal Marcello declared: "Here we are."
> Then Michelangelo said to him: "My Lord, above these windows in the vault, which will be made of travertine, are to go three more."
> "But you never told us that," the cardinal remarked. And then Michelangelo announced: "I'm not and I don't intend to be obliged to discuss with your Eminence or anyone else what I ought or intend to do. Your duty is to collect the money and guard it against thieves, and you must leave the task of designing the building to me."
> Then he turned to the Pope and added: "Holy Father, you know what my earnings are from this enterprise, and you know that unless my labours bring me spiritual satisfaction I am wasting all my time and work."
> The Pope, who loved him, put his hand on Michelangelo's shoulder and said:
> "Both your soul and your body will profit, never fear."

PLATE II

After Michelangelo's death in 1564, St. Peter's changed little. It exists today as essentially his building, a simplified version of the Bramante-Sangallo plan, with an exterior of flowing curves and planes, punctuated by four corner towers that reflect Bramante's four piers within. Between 1586 and 1593 the impressive building progressed in stately allegiance to Michelangelo's plan. The dome was built by Giacomo della Porta and Domenico Fontana. The height of the inner shell of the dome of St. Peter's was increased by one third of that projected by Michelangelo. Della Porta felt that the calm and unity of Bramante's dome manifested themselves clearly and exquisitely in the broad colonnade and the rings supporting its springing. That the drum was the most important feature and floated over the tomb of the chief apostle like a noble crown, surmounted only by the necessary ceiling, which, in the form of an elegant saucer-dome, rested lightly on the colonnade. Michelangelo divided the colonnade into single buttresses with paired columns, thereby increasing the verticality, but also the load. His dome, furthermore, is much more massive. The model of Michelangelo's design in the Vatican Museum shows that the internal dome was designed to be hemispherical, but the external to be as built. It is not certain whether this change was intended by Michelangelo or brought about by his followers, but it is interesting that compared to the engraving of Dupérac, the existing dome is much more elegant and lifted and suggests an increased admiration for the Gothic characteristic of the Baroque period.

Carlo Maderno's task was to solve the problem of integrating the old St. Peter's with the building by Michelangelo, whilst considering the practical needs of accommodating the Benediction Loggia and space for the increasingly large crowds coming to Rome. It must not be forgotten that the Easter blessing of the crowds by the Pope was an essential of religious life in Rome. Maderno's debt to Michelangelo is clear, but the façade is also similar to his own at Sta. Susanna; what is immediately striking is how palatial this colossal façade is. The Pope was to stand above a relief of Christ giving the keys to St. Peter, and above him statues of apostles break the line of the long narthex, almost like a *galleria* of a cinquecento palace. His achievement is to have created an entirely original façade quite in the spirit of the existing building, and to have linked the old basilica to Michelangelo's centralised building without detracting from the grandeur of the dome.

The story of St. Peter's does not end with Maderno's façade. In 1629 Bernini took over completion of the façade and the piazza to surround it. His was the final emotional, symbolic and architectural conclusion to St. Peter's. Greuter's engraving shows that in Maderno's time a piazza with central obelisk was intended to focus the attention of observers on the building. But Bernini's colonnade opened up the cathedral to its worshippers, embracing the populace in its curving arms and, practically, providing a large gathering place for Papal addresses. It is a far cry from Bramante's concept of a cathedral as an isolated structure commanding all the buildings around it, but it is an equally powerful, if more rhetorical, statement. As originally built it would have controlled the visitor's view of the building;

the façade could only be glimpsed when the viewer was standing in the right position to see it in relation to the dome and the grandeur of the whole building. The architecture of the cathedral and of the Vatican Palace were now perfectly integrated, although subsequently the effect has been spoiled by the opening up of the Via della Conciliazione (1939-50). It is to the credit of Bramante, Michelangelo and Bernini and of the ruling popes, that the cathedral should exist in such an impressive and apparently coherent form, whilst representing Renaissance, Mannerist and Baroque ideals, and being the result of an enormous number of designs and theories.

16 Detail from a page of Leonardo da Vinci's
    notebooks showing a centralised church
    encircled by small chapels and a colonnaded
    temple redolent of Bramante's later
    Tempietto in Rome.

uno porto alquella larghezza enullo
no. leparti difotto era alpiano delterre
forma. ellera prima fcompartita intre

Cragli ancora
molti hor
namenti
doro &
dar

m dicofe. Dorace tutte erano. Cragli
bronzo maramiglio fiffimi auedere iquali
doue cheneluano della circunferenza
era molti hornamenti doro & dargenti

18 Caradosso's foundation medal of 1506
    which shows, almost certainly, the west
    front of Bramante's first project.

19a Engraving by Salamanca of the beautifully
     decorated giant model by Labacco of 1548,
     from the designs of Antonio Sangallo.

19b Section of the Labacco model showing the
     structure of the dome and the unsatisfactory
     relationship of the different parts of the
     Cathedral.

PAVLI III PONT MAX
LIBERALITATI
DICATVM

ANTONIVS · S · GALLI INVENTOR
ANTONIVS LABACCVS EIVS DISCIP
EFFECTOR

20 Michelangelo's last model as engraved by
Etienne Dupérac in 1569 clearly showing his
early dome as more squat than that
executed.

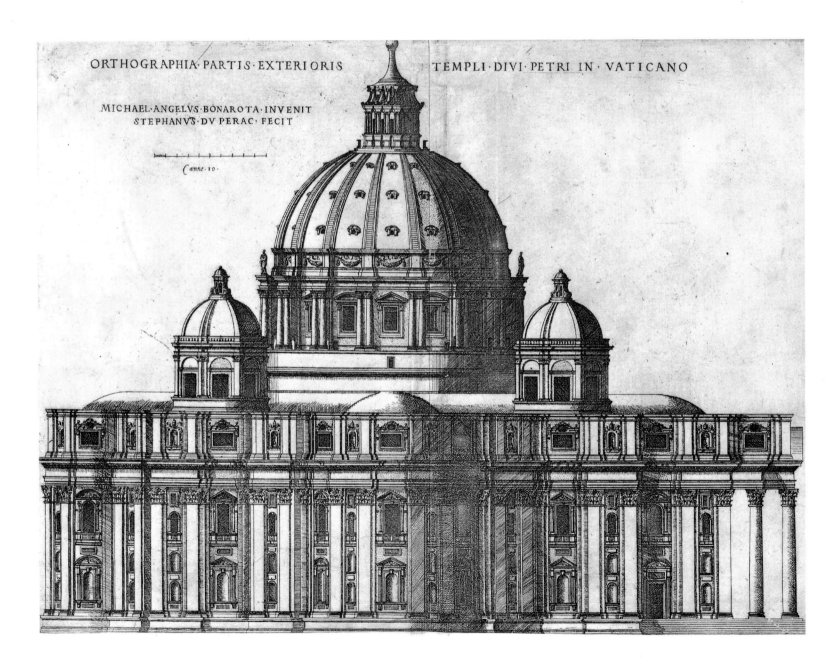

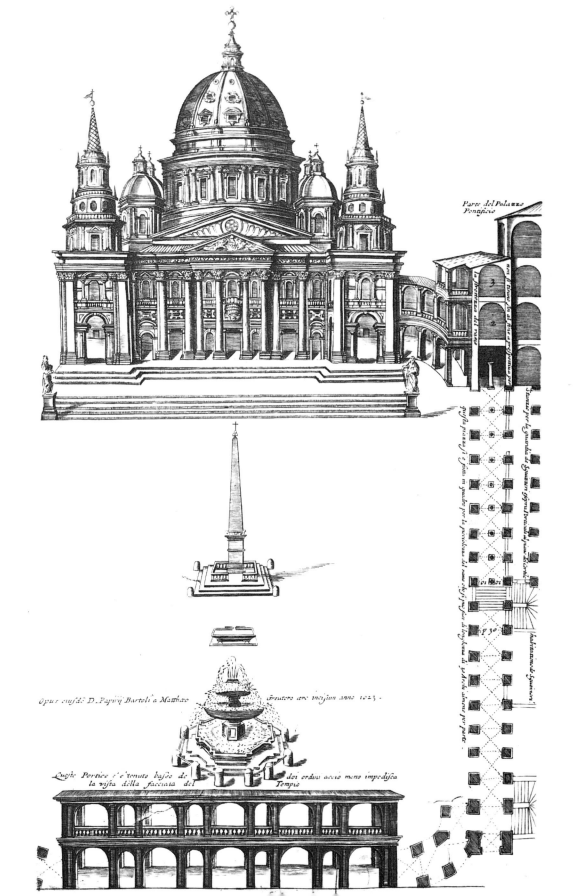

21 One resolution for the piazza of St. Peter's which begins to give the façade greater emphasis by using statues and a central obelisk. The Cathedral itself is a delightfully inaccurate mixture of the various façade schemes.

22 Greuter's fine engraving of Maderno's façade with projected campanili, 1613.

BASILICA DI S. PIETRO IN VATICANO

23 Engraving by Falda from Rossi's *Nuovo Teatro*, 1665, showing the completed St. Peter's and Bernini's.

DRAWINGS AFTER SOME OF THE CENTRALISED PLANS FOR
ST. PETER'S, ROME.

24 Sangallo's plan based on Bramante's most
complex geometric design, The Parchment
Plan. The massive scheme was designed to
incorporate the ancient basilica inside the
central space.

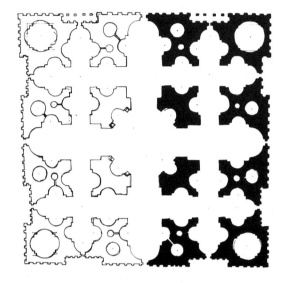

26 Bramante's favoured plan for St. Peter's.

27 Michelangelo's central plan which clearly
derives from Bramante's beginnings but
which adds tension and massiveness.

25 Probably Giuliano da ?
a simple, open, domed

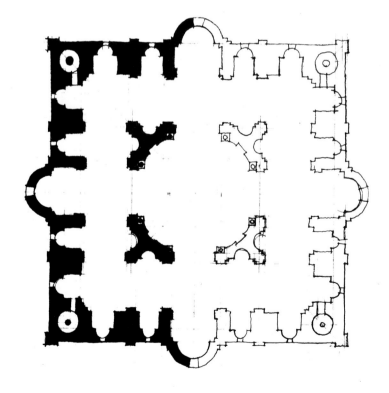

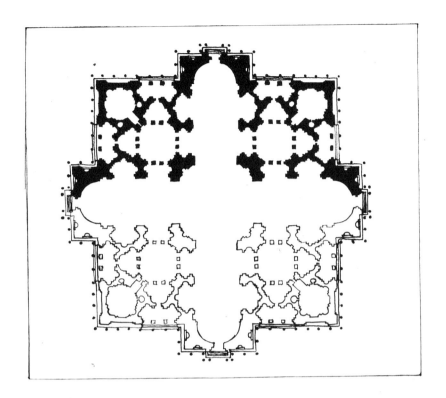

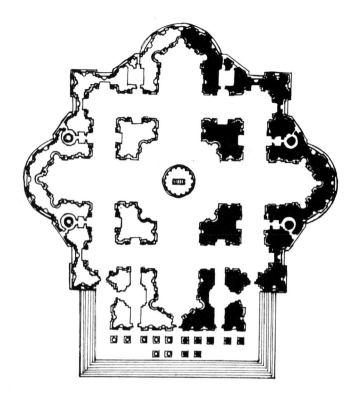

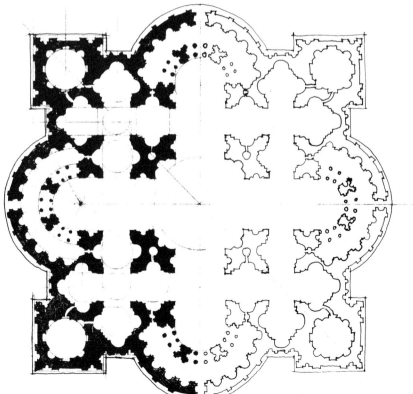

28 Baldassare Peruzzi's sensitive completion of Bramante's Greek cross. The lighter shading of the drawing shows Peruzzi's additions – a satisfying piece of design.

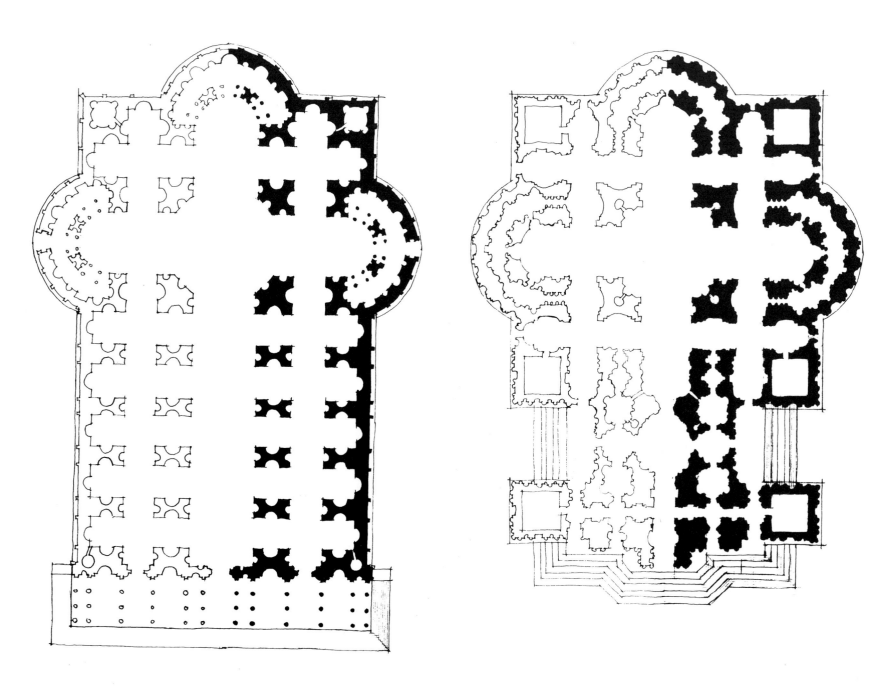

29 **R**aphael's Latin cross with colonnaded
façade of 1514 is disappointingly unoriginal.

30 **A**ntonio Cordini's plan which relates
closely to the model by Antonio da Sangallo.

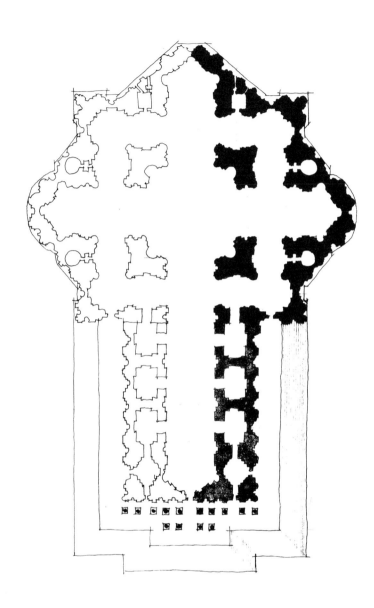

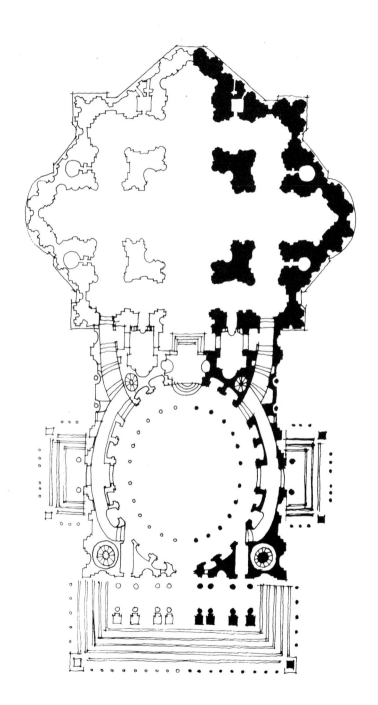

31 Domenico Fontana's design – Longitudinal and uncontroversial.

32 The two parts of the church in Fausto Rughesi's project are linked by a strange colonnaded atrium made up of two half-circles. The effect is of an oval – a favourite form for Baroque architects.

3. MILAN CATHEDRAL 'A WORK OF SUCH FAME AND IMPORTANCE'

*T*his chapter will examine the towers, spires and pinnacles proposed and rejected for the west front of one church. Milan, unlike St. Paul's in London, is not a case of one entire design rejected and rearranged in favour of another, nor does it illustrate a progressive growth from a central idea, like St. Peter's in Rome. Milan Cathedral had the misfortune to be almost complete in an age when its style, Gothic, went out of fashion. The problem was not one of building a new church without the dictates of a predecessor, but of finishing a vast and imposing structure in a way both appropriate to the body of the church and acceptable to the changed tastes of the post-medieval world.

From the start, Milan had been conceived as a monumental building, of international importance. It suffered, however, from the conflicting enthusiasms to be found amongst those in charge of its construction and furthermore, was to be built in a style that was really more at home north of the Alps. Although the cathedral was eventually built with relative ease, its early history was dogged by technical and aesthetic controversy.

Work began in 1387, under the direction of Simone da Orsenigo. Almost immediately, however, foreign experts were called in for consultation. Each one proposed to build a different sort of cathedral. The French master, Nicholas of Bonaventure, proposed a church in classic French proportions. Heinrich Parler, in charge from 1391-92, suggested a structure of towering height. The Italians, supported by the mathematician, Gabriele Stornacolo, favoured the broad and low proportions of classical geometry. Only by 1401 had contention subsided sufficiently to allow work to continue and in 1418, Pope Martin V consecrated the high altar.

The body of the church is a *tour de force* of late Gothic, a complex and eclectic hybrid, covered on its exterior surface by a profusion of carved ornament. As its construction progressed through the fifteenth century however, the architecture of the Renaissance was to become increasingly dominant – the great families of Milan were building themselves grand classical palaces, not Gothic ones. Nor could other Italian cathedrals really serve as models for Milan's façade. For all their beauty, the façades of Siena and Florence lack the lightness and verticality demanded by the exuberant Gothic of Milan.

Rudolf Wittkower, in his marvellous analysis both of Milan and of Bologna, in *Gothic versus Classic*, suggested that the façade of the cathedral was probably not given serious consideration until after around 1530, as in 1534 there was the first request from the Council that creative attention should be focused on the west front. In 1537 the architect Vincenzo Seregni submitted a design. Its precise elevation is unknown but as he himself wrote, it conformed with the intentions of the founders of the cathedral, so this implies a design that echoed the Gothic of the rest of the building. Seregni was not at this point the project's official architect, merely one who had submitted designs. In 1547 he was made sole architect to the cathedral, taking charge in 1555 at the death of Christophoro Lombardo. Although he remained in office until dismissed in 1567, his influence on the cathedral was not great.

More crucial to the progress was the appointment of Carlo Borromeo as Cardinal Archbishop of Milan in 1560. At 22, he was perhaps a little young for the task but had the inestimable advantage of being nephew of Pope Pius IV. He rapidly became one of the leading churchmen of the Counter-Reformation and was canonised in 1610. His wide-ranging dynamism was only brought to bear on Milan in 1565 when he came to live in his archdiocese.

Borromeo turned his energies to many things, not least of them architecture. In 1557 he published a small book *Instructions for Ecclesiastical Buildings*, designed to relate the decrees of the Council of Trent (the great Counter-Reformation gathering of the Catholic church which formulated the attitude held by the Papacy to the new circumstances of the Reformation) to architecture. It is irritating that he did not comment more upon style: had he done so we could be more sure of his intentions for the church which was to be the seat of the great Counter-Reformation archdiocese of northern Italy. However, his determined and loyal patronage of a new man shows the sort of architect he wanted. Rather unusually he chose a celebrated painter, Pellegrino Tibaldi, also known as Pellegrino Pellegrini. Pellegrini had spent three years in Rome from 1549 to 1553 when he fell very much under the spell of Michelangelo. Borromeo met him later in Bologna and called him to Milan in 1564 as architect to the cathedral.

Pellegrini had almost twenty years of favour in Milan and many fittings were executed for the cathedral under his regime; the side altars, the main altar, the baptistry, presbytery, pulpits and many other parts of the church were completed in the new, classical style. But the most important aspect of the church, the façade, did not progress rapidly. Pellegrini made designs for it in an uncompromisingly classical style; he was intending to break away from the Gothic of the rest of the church and to have a façade dominated by huge Corinthian columns in the style of Michelangelo's St. Peter's, Rome. It was a step in a new direction but one that was fraught with intrigue. After the architect's death in 1596, his worked-up drawing of the façade was passed from one cathedral architect to another, finally coming into the possession of Antonio Mario Corbetta, architect from 1606 to 1609. His was not the happiest of relationships with his client body and he was dismissed. When he had gone, Pellegrini's design had vanished. Asked about its disappearance Corbetta claimed to have returned it to the archives, a response which was not believed. Poor Corbetta was then threatened with excommunication if the missing drawing did not reappear but even this failed to produce the design. In 1611 a summons from Rome was served on the luckless architect, though no explanation was forthcoming as to why he should so stubbornly wish to keep a predecessor's design. Finally, perhaps in response to legal threats, a damaged and repaired Pellegrini drawing materialised mysteriously in the archives. The archivist wisely instructed his carpenter to make a model from it, but to no avail, it disappeared before this could take place and was never seen again.

The vanishing trick was probably a deliberate move by the cathedral authorities. They had never liked the architect, because of the high-handed way in which Borromeo had imposed him upon them, and they had constantly interfered with his working. Opposition was spear-headed by architect and engineer Martino Bassi, who manipulated the Council into a serious investigation of Pellegrini's alleged misconduct. Exonerated at the intervention of Borromeo his patron, Pellegrini had to face further criticism in the form of a book published by Bassi in 1572. To give weight to his cause, Bassi enlisted the support of Palladio, Vignola and Vasari. Again he was protected by Borromeo, the whole dispute turning now entirely on power politics rather than on genuine arguments of inefficiency.

Borromeo's support was vital to the architect and when that august patron died in 1584 the days of protection were over, and Pellegrini soon accepted the very flattering invitation from Philip II of Spain to work on the Escorial in Madrid. In Milan, though Bassi at last had the freedom in the cathedral's affairs that he desired, and though he suggested with some degree of force that the façade be got underway, little actually happened, mainly because Bassi's façade designs met with papal opposition.

Thus the cathedral hovered on the brink of being given a classical façade, but nothing materialised. The seventeenth-century response to the cathedral's problem followed this lead. Pellegrini's importance lay in turning the cathedral away from a Gothic conclusion towards a classical one. Most important of all, in August 1583 the contracts were signed for the construction of the foundations for the main portal according to Pellegrini's design, and in 1609 it was again formally decided to proceed according to this particular classical scheme.

The façade design seemed to have been sorted out. But problems arose over the upper tier; the huge marble columns required were proving impossible to transport whole – they kept breaking. Such difficulties naturally held up the building programme. An engraving of 1735, dolefully commemorating the funeral of the Queen of Sardinia, shows that Pellegrini's façade had been

started but hardly more than that; only the five main portals and the windows above the north door had been executed, together with the truncated length of pilasters again on the north flank of the church. These pilasters, rising through two storeys, are important because they seem to show deviation from Pellegrini's scheme since he had intended half columns and not pilasters. This indicates that the changes were made to the design almost certainly by Francesco Ricchino, a member of the commission advising the church. Ricchino's alterations to Pellegrini's design for the upper part of the church combined to give it a more Baroque feel to it, the result of his stay in Rome earlier in the century, when he was most impressed by works such as Maderno's Sta. Susanna. Ricchino made several designs, one of which is important because, with its unbroken entablature between the two storeys, it separates the building very firmly into two parts, a marked contrast to the integration that Pellegrini would have favoured. What he did not suggest, perhaps because it was unlikely that he would have found it easy to convince the authorities of its usefulness, was the addition of campanili or spires of any kind. His façades, whether from the early 1600s or as late as the 1630s when he was finally made cathedral architect, show determination to control the vertical emphasis of the building. The cathedral is divided horizontally, and while the pediment is adorned by statues, they are not statues which function as bristling pinnacles, they are too few. Instead Ricchino gives us a façade that is controlled and classical, not one that at all implies a lofty Gothic cathedral behind it.

Ricchino was by no means the only architect in the early seventeenth century to propose designs for the façade. On the contrary, there survive innumerable schemes by others with greater or lesser degrees of talent. One, now anonymous, is marked by its use of rather tortured-looking obelisks, which flare like brands up and down the left of the façade, giving a visual link to the Gothic spikiness behind it, but at the expense of logic and balance. This façade, probably the work of an enthusiastic amateur, can hardly have received serious consideration. More authoritative was a scheme, possibly by Lelio Buzzi, who worked as acting architect to the cathedral from 1591 to 1603. This has almost no ornament on the roof line but veers too far towards heaviness with its lumpy niches, inelegant volutes and over-elaborate use of depressed panelling to break up the wall surface. It is at once severe and cluttered.

What these and other obscure designs show is the enthusiasm at the time for the same basic scheme, classical, un-towered, with much use of giant pilasters. Work, as we have seen, began to these general specifications and progressed slowly. Ricchino was appointed to an important position similar to that of Clerk of the Works when he was only twenty-one years old, and was associated closely with the cathedral for thirty-five years. Like Pellegrini he enjoyed the continued and very loyal patronage of a Borromeo, in this case Cardinal Federico Borromeo, who like his forebear protected his architect in times of criticism and acrimonious debate. History seemed to repeat itself, the more so when Ricchino was left without his patron at the death of Borromeo. Like his predecessor, he was now defenceless and in July 1638, seven years after Borromeo's death, he was cursorily dismissed and forbidden to go near the project. This was distressing for the architect, but fatal for his design: the classical schemes that he had so diligently evolved were brought into question.

This change of tack came about because the Council had decided on a new architect, Carlo Buzzi, son of Lelio Buzzi. Carlo was in office for twenty years 1648 to 1668. He might have seemed a surprising choice, having executed few buildings before his appointment. This did not stop him however, from planning an architectural revolution. Three major designs by him exist, and they share one feature – an uncompromising return to Gothic. The most elaborate, dated around 1645, shows a cathedral with classical portals inherited from Pellegrini and classical windows but otherwise completely Gothic: Gothic panelling runs up the face of the church with hardly any horizontal interruption. The outline of the façade is a continuous sequence of stumpy pinnacles, punctuated by the occasional vigorous spirelet. Most Gothic of all, the façade is flanked by two tall towers outside the aisles, complete with Gothic windows and topped by fetching spiral-staircase in the form of steeples. It was a complete reversal of earlier policy and a momentous one.

The Council was in no doubt as to the enormity of the change and, to understand more fully the decision, asked that Pellegrini's, Ricchino's and Buzzi's schemes be engraved and discussed seriously. In December 1646, Buzzi reported on his choice of design: his was, he said, a compound of Roman and Gothic architecture as he taken care that the part executed in classical style and that to be built should be compatible – not a consideration that had seized his predecessors. In elaborating his point, Buzzi went on to say that the classical schemes were too high and would hide the upper part of the cathedral surely, he said, its most beautiful and ornate part. This too was a new approach. Earlier architects would have shuddered at the thought of so much ill-designed Gothic work freely displayed. Now it was easier to appreciate. But Buzzi went further: in advocating his mixture of inherited classical doorways and Gothic pinnacles Buzzi reminded his audience of the interior of the cathedral. Here, he said, were classical tombs, altars and other fittings in a Gothic setting, a mixture which was to him in no way offensive.

This detached appreciation that could leap the seemingly impenetrable barriers of style was wholly new. Gone was the partisan obsession with all things classical with a concomitant loathing of Gothic. Buzzi's ideas combined both practicality, there was no need to demolish extant work – with a determination to show how admirable was the church as a whole. His seeing the church as one piece of work was new and easy to appreciate. Unlike his predecessors, he exhibited an engraving of the side of the church showing how well his façade would fit the rest of the building, the aim being not to hide the Gothic body of the church but to celebrate it. His designs were given one further elaboration. It was decided in 1653 to introduce Gothic windows to replace the classical windows over the main portal.

When Buzzi died in 1568 he was replaced by one who had already tried to usurp him and to impose his own, perhaps crazy, Gothic ideas on the scheme: this was Francesco Castelli. Castelli had caused Buzzi enormous trouble by submitting Gothic designs and compelling the council's attentions to them. Buzzi, and rather surprisingly, the dismissed Ricchino, were asked to comment. Both were unimpressed, but the serious consideration given the newcomer's project made it important that both Buzzi's and Castelli's schemes be engraved. Castelli attracted praise in Milan for introducing a *new* Gothic, a Gothic appropriate to a classical age, a Gothic which seemed consistent with classical laws of proportion. His was in fact a Gothic which was subservient to classical architecture, one deeply aware of its superior style. Buzzi's on the other hand was the *ancient* Gothic: which was the better? To settle the issue, it was felt necessary to ask outsiders, the most important of which was the great architect Bernini.

Bernini however was irritatingly inconclusive. Castelli's church he said 'pleased me very much indeed' but before finishing 'a work of such fame and importance' he should make another design adding campanili. Bernini veered towards Castelli by dint of almost ignoring Buzzi, but the matter was still unsettled. Further comment was therefore occasioned by the publication around 1656 of a pamphlet containing many of the designs for the cathedral and this prompted a longer remark from Bernini. Bernini's enthusiasm for Castelli's scheme arose because it was in a Gothic style tailored for those who knew classical form and proportions. This point of view was voluminously argued and must have profoundly shocked the authorities in Milan, who were expecting confirmation of their view, that Buzzi's design was acceptable. In any case, the immediate effect was to cause a halt to the erection of Buzzi's schemes which had previously seemed so certain of execution. As with the vacillation that had surrounded Pellegrini's work, the hiatus produced a few works of well-intentioned architectural idiocy, which this time tried to combine features of Castelli with elements from the less disciplined recesses of the imagination. However, these anonymous schemes merely act as eyebrow-raising comments on the ever-changing demands of the project.

This sequence of unsatisfactory changes brought the building to a complete standstill. By 1658 the façade had been under fairly active consideration for 150 years: purely classical designs, almost purely Gothic designs, hybrid designs, all had poured from architect's pens, all, it now transpired, to no avail. Now a long period of inertia settled upon the project to last well into the eighteenth century, dented but not interrupted by vague attempts to persuade Bernini himself to come to Milan in 1665.

First signs of movement occurred in 1732 when the authorities decided once more to try and complete the façade. The Piedmontese architect, Juvarra, was invited to submit his solution, and, although he could not attend it, an important meeting to discuss the issue nonetheless took place in 1733. At this meeting three proposals were put forward: to build in a classical style, to build in a Gothic one, to mix the two. Eventually it was decided that a mixture would suit – i.e. the same decision as that arrived at in the seventeenth century. Juvarra's resultant designs have vanished but, just as on earlier occasions, the attention and indecision surrounding the projects stirred the gifted (and those who so considered themselves) to put pen to paper. A rush of hybrid Gothic schemes, ranging from the inventive to the mutant, appeared.

Among the more interesting was one by Antonio Maria Vertemate Cotognola, which shamelessly mixed Buzzi and Castelli motifs with Baroque indulgences, such as a dome over the west end of the church. Since Cotognola's widow was paid a sum on his death, by the authorities, it must have had some serious consideration. Nevertheless it, like all its antecedents and contemporaries, got nowhere. The same, sadly, is true of the vigorous scheme by Bernardo Vittone, one of the greatest Italian architects of the time, which was eventually published in 1766. This, like Buzzi's, was intended to impress with campanili separated by a very sinewy, Gothic main façade, complete with large French Gothic windows. A feeling of Rococo resplendence is evident in the fluid mobility of this design in contrast to that of his successors such as Giulio Galliori's of *c.*1786-87. Galliori's design was, as Wittkower said, of a dry, temperate Gothic 'so reasonable that it makes one almost yawn'. This brings us to the end of the eighteenth century. In a period four times longer than the amount of time it took Wren to plan and build completely a new St. Paul's in London, Milan Cathedral had remained without a fitting entrance, while literally hundreds of designs were rejected. Was there any possibility that the situation would change?

In 1787 this seemed unlikely yet ten years later events of an unecclesiastical nature intervened. By 1797 Napoleon Bonaparte, then in control of Lombardy, began to pay attention to this eyesore in Milan and in 1805, by this time Emperor, he demanded its completion. He was not to be disobeyed; nor were the long-winded cathedral authorities to have much say in the matter. Under Carlo Amati a façade was built which used elements of Buzzi's church and elements of Pellegrini's (the doorways). It is as a compromise, albeit one not lacking in elegance, that it exists today but only as the result of one final instance of inertia. The nineteenth century was not usually one to tolerate architectural unorthodoxy, and the Gothic-classical blur of the newly completed façade was an offence to the stylistically pure at heart. In 1884 an opportunity to rectify this presented itself when Aristide de Togni left his fortune for the reconstruction of the façade. An international competition was announced, and entries from one hundred and twenty architects were soon received. In 1887, fifteen were selected for the final competition. From Britain, the practice of Pugin and Pugin submitted a scheme, but it was too late. Entries came from France, Germany and elsewhere and the most successful British entrant, Daniel Brade sent a beautiful watercolour design now in the RIBA. But the winner, after second submission, was Giuseppe Brentano. To the surprise of no one with knowledge of such a competition, his winning design remained firmly unexecuted. The cathedral he proposed would have had a vast Gothic window, reminiscent of those round the east end of the church, as its central feature rearing above the main doorways. It would have been a façade entirely in keeping with the bulk of the cathedral, but one not redolent of the troubled history of the project. As it is, the survival of the early nineteenth-century façade, which in itself combined features of several preceding centuries, is a quiet indication of the problems that one cathedral faced in achieving completion. Brentano's design, like its antecedents, remains just a beguiling paper cathedral.

PLATE III

33 Pellegrino Pellegrini was responsible for a
classical design for Milan Cathedral's
façade.

34 An anonymous contribution: spiky and
staccato, it seems to echo the Gothic
buttresses of the body of the building.

35 A classical design, possibly by Lelio Buzzi,
of the late sixteenth century.

36 Milan Cathedral at the time of the funeral
of the Queen of Sardinia showing the
unfinished state of the façade.

37 Francesco Maria Ricchino's Façade, showing the influence of his stay in Rome.

38 A contrast to the classicism of previous architects, Carlo Buzzi's splendid Gothic façade was flanked by elegant campanili.

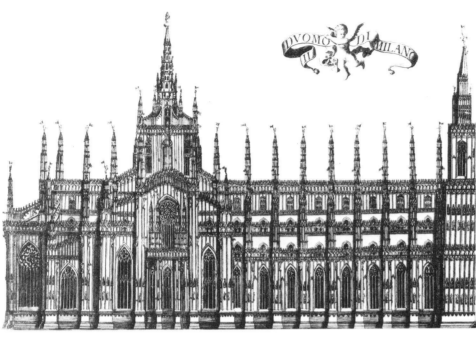

39 The side elevation of Buzzi's façade, showing how it related to the rest of the building.

41 Antonio Maria Vertemate Cotognola proposed a Gothic façade incorporating a dome.

40 A later anonymous Gothic scheme for Milan.

42 Bernardo Vittone's façade of 1746.

43 The 1888 competition winner: Giuseppe Brentano.

44 Milan Cathedral as built.

4. A DRAMATIC REVOLT: THE BAROQUE IN ITALY

*B*y the mid-sixteenth century the architecture of the Renaissance did not satisfy. Perhaps its reasoned classicism was insufficient to express the restless mood of Italy, perhaps architects felt that Bramante and others had reached the ultimate artistic expression in their work in Rome? Certainly the new religious orders of the Counter-Reformation seemed to need different kinds of architecture to suit their aims and ideals.

Whatever the reasons, there emerged from under the shadow of St. Peter's a new style, called by contemporaries *'stilo moderno'*, which was neither antique nor Gothic, the *'stilo tedesco'*. The words often used by Vasari to describe it: *'bizarro' 'capriccioso'*, *'stravagante'* show how it contrasted with Renaissance sobriety, and immediately bring to mind the masters of high Baroque, Borromini and Guarini. The *'stilo moderno'* does not begin, however, to define what we now call the Baroque period which spans an enormous variety of styles from the monumental Baroque of Rome to the eighteenth-century Rococo of Germany.

Examination of unexecuted church designs of this period makes the aims and the progress of this style clearer, but it is first and foremost a pleasurable process. The nature of the greatest Baroque design, its painterly illusions of movement, its bizarre symbolism and elusive, constantly changing lines, its digressions from the rules of architecture, whilst retaining tense geometrical control, is such that the architecture is hardly less exciting when it is reduced to one dimension although it is often less overwhelming.

The Gesù in Rome of 1568 was indisputably one of the most influential architectural statements of the Renaissance. It can even be argued that Giacomo Barozzi da Vignola's longitudinal plan was a large part of the impetus behind St. Peter's final form. It is not our purpose here to discuss details of Vignola's contribution, suffice it to say he found a perfect solution to the combination of dome and longitudinal nave. What is interesting to us is that the return to longitudinal form brought with it an emphasis on the façade; it was to develop into an architectural showpiece in the hands of Baroque architects and, as we shall clearly see in Borromini's façade of the Oratorio of S. Filippo Neri, Rome, did not necessarily bear any relation to the interior. It was often too the only part of the church to be faced in stone; thus into the Gesù's façade we may read much of the architectural thinking of the day. It is fascinating to examine the differences between Vignola's own façade design and the façade executed by his successor to the project in 1573, Giacomo della Porta, since in some ways they epitomise the change from Renaissance to Baroque.

The Gesù was to be the main church of the newly-founded order of the Jesuits, headed by St. Ignatius Loyola, who had been living and preaching in absurdly cramped conditions in Rome. Their need was great but their funds lacking, so the commission ended up being a compromise between the requirements of the Jesuits under St. Ignatius and St. Francis Borgia, who wanted a large cross plan with good acoustics, lots of side chapels and a façade flanked by two towers, in the manner of Sangallo's model of St. Peter's, and Cardinal Alessandro Farnese who desired an elegant 'modern' building, and who supplied most of the money. The Jesuit order prided itself on asceticism and hard work and this must surely be taken into account as an influence on the aesthetics of the whole church, including the final choice of the façade. The façade shown in the foundation model of 1568 was of planar simplicity; this was followed by further designs in 1569 and 1570 by Vignola, culminating in the one illustrated, which was engraved by Mario Cartaro in 1573. Significantly, the inscription on the frieze celebrates Cardinal Alessandro Farnese and not the Jesuits. But this design was rejected by the Cardinal too despite its attempts at palatial decoration. One might presume that the Jesuits desire for simplicity had finally won over Farnese's own tastes but in fact della Porta also replaced Vignola on the building of the Farnese palace, so it may simply have been an aesthetic choice by both patrons. The two façades follow a formula: they are in two storeys – the bottom one corresponding to the height of the chapel and the top corresponding to the height of the nave and flanked by two volutes. This is the formula of Alberti's Sta. Maria Novella in Florence and many others, yet one that is shown in the Baroque period to offer enormous variety. Within it, Vignola suggests a rectangular centre with subsidiary wings where the horizontal and vertical features are carefully balanced and the richly harmonious ornamentation of statues and niches articulate the façade for a pleasing staccato effect. Della Porta's façade creates a dramatic crescendo. The main portal is accentuated by the intervention of a pediment within a pediment, and the upward thrust is emphasized by drawing all the niches into the central area, leaving the outer wings bare, and by making the medallion in the top storey pediment oval rather than circular. By breaking through it with what appear to be continuations of the pilasters, the independent parts have been subordinated to the whole. The difference between the façades is defined even by the volutes. Vignola's volutes are unornamented links between the two storeys: they seem primarily functional like those on Bramante's dome of St. Peter's. Della Porta's decorated scrolls, a female head carrying an Ionic capital, sweep dramatically up and add dignity with their weight, as do his double pilasters. They seem to tie the whole design together although their curves are soft. The latter façade clearly derives from Vignola yet somehow simplifies and strengthens his ideas. Completed in 1575, it was enormously influential on Baroque façades as a whole.

Francesco Borromini (1599-1695) could be described as one of della Porta's successors in Rome. But Borromini was a man of quite extraordinary genius and personality, in a sense successor to none. Primarily a stone carver, he had worked until he was thirty on the decorative details of St. Peter's. His talent as a draughtsman was never lost and his drawing, from the Albertina, of the Oratorio of S. Filippo Neri is quite exquisite. The lines are vibrant with energy, lending movement to the architecture itself; his mathematical accuracy and artistry are perfectly in balance and the changing lines are not uncertain. Unfortunately for us, Borromini's peculiar temperament (according to E.B. Passeri in *Vitae de Pittori, Scultori and Architetti . . . in Roma dal 1640 fino al 1673* he was celibate, deeply religious, frightened people and dressed in funereal black like a Spaniard, only sporting red garters and rosettes on his shoes) led him to commit suicide and while he was dying he destroyed many drawings, the quantity and quality of which hardly bears thinking about.

The differences observable between the two engravings of the façade of the Oratorio are not great but, since they can be easily attributed to Borromini's patrons, they are interesting historically. He was chosen for the project in 1637 by one of the fathers of the new order of Oratorians, Virgilio Spada. He and his brother Cardinal Bernadino were protégés of Pope Urban VIII and connoisseurs of architecture. Borromini's talent had been noticed while he was working in the Cardinal's palace and on the church of S. Carlo alle Quattro Fontane, Rome, in 1634 where he won a good name for himself amongst the Discalced Trinitarians for the cheapness of his plans as well as for their revolutionary, tormented, attenuated sensuality, the architectural equivalent of the paintings of El Greco.

The Oratorians prided themselves on their pious and simple way of life of culture and learning and they required from Borromini a reflection of this in their Oratory for musical performances, a library and accommodation for the brothers. The façade of the Oratory was to relate to Fausto Rughesi's façade of Sta. Maria in Vallicella of 1605, which was on the della Porta model and stood next-door to the proposed Oratory. The architect was issued with instructions not to compete with the church façade, not to use columns or stone facings (the brick side-bays of the unexecuted design suggest that the proposed central panel was in stone), but it seems reasonable to assume that this was also behind the rejection of the early design's salamanic door portals and elaborate symbolic finials.

If less elaborate, the completed design retained the disturbing tension of the slow curve, the inverted 'S' shapes created by the door and its niche above and the new, combined, straight and curved pediment. Borromini even revived a type of very smooth classical brickwork to overcome the restrictions on the use of stone. It is an entirely expressive façade yet one created by very careful interplay of geometric shapes; throughout his career Borromini never relinquished this control. For him, 'The Great Book of Nature is written in the language of mathematics, and its characters, circles, and other geometric figures'. His career was a continual process of original synthesis of internal architectural sources and geometric experiment. The effects, though sometimes bizarre, are always exciting.

Surprisingly, Borromini was to find heirs for his genius in Piedmont. A detailed engraving of his lantern of S. Ivo alla Sapienza, an apparently wild invention, gives us the perfect link to Piedmont since its influence on Guarini's centrally-planned churches and Juvarra's lantern on the Superga of 1717 must be acknowledged. Its spiral ramp ascends like a symbol for the Tower of Wisdom, ending in the Flame of Truth and supporting a cross on an orb; a beautiful progression of contrasting sculptural forms. It is also redolent of the Ziggurats, the Babylonian or Assyrian temple towers. This must have been a starting point for the wonderful towers of Guarini (and even perhaps for the spires of Wren's city churches) just as the illusionary lighting effects in the Oratorio were a stimulus for Guarini's later dramatically lit domes.

We are specially lucky in having a wealth of documents on Peidmontese architecture executed or not: not only Guarini's *Architettura Civile* but also Vittone's *Istruzzioni Elementari* and *Diversi* as well as a lot of surviving drawings by Juvarra. There is not scope in this book to do them justice, but in the case of Guarini they are particularly valuable, since they compensate for the sad fate of many of his executed buildings. They also place the bizarre Capella della Ss. Sindoni and Lorenzo in Turin in the context of a whole architectural style, rather than individual flashes of genius as they might otherwise appear. Guarino Guarini was born in Modena in 1624 and entered the Theatine Order at fifteen. He studied for the priesthood for four years in Rome when he must have seen and admired the churches of Borromini, returning to Modena to lecture on philosophy and then moving to Messina to teach philosophy and mathematics. This intellectual background is important to his architecture as it was to Borromini. In Messina he is known to have designed two churches, one the chapel of Sta. Annunciata which was tragically destroyed in an earthquake in 1908 and about which we know little, and a rather dull hexagonal church.

The next years took him to Paris where his Ste. Anne-la-Royale with its pagoda-like exterior, undulating façade and kidney-shaped windows show the beginning of his true quality. This too was sadly demolished in 1823. It was then likely that Guarini travelled to Spain and Portugal and absorbed some of the Moorish influences there as well as the influences of the great Gothic cathedrals in France and Spain. At this time too, he probably designed the church of Sta. Maria della Providenza in Lisbon which was destroyed in an earthquake of 1755. Guarini was not unique to be travelling so far abroad: by the second half of the seventeenth century the catastrophic financial and political decline of the Barberinis and the uninspired phase of building in Rome contrasted with the growing power of the Holy Roman Empire and France in the north. French architecture had been given an enormous boost by François Mansard and he must be seen as the second most influential contemporary architect on Guarini after Borromini; his brilliant displays of skill in cut stone,

PLATE IV
PLATE V

for example in the vaults of the Château at Blois of the 1630s, must have contributed to Guarini's virtuoso displays later on; Guarini who claims of geometric projection that 'It is absolutely necessary to the architect, even though it is little known in Italian architecture, and is conspicuously adopted on many occasions only by the French'. Moreover an appreciation of Gothic architecture seems to have blown like a fresh wind into the minds of architects. His description of Gothic architecture in the *Architettura Civile* is totally revealing:

> The Romans wanted their buildings to be strong, and to look it. The Goths, on the other hand, admired extreme height and slenderness: they wanted their churches to appear weak, so that it seemed a miracle that they could stand up. Therefore one will see a gigantic bell-tower set on extremely frail columns; arches that bend back over the springing, which itself hangs in the air without resting on the column below; little towers, completely perforated, that terminate in steep pyramids; windows extremely tall (or high up); and vaults without flanks. The Goths even had the daring to set the corners of high towers above the crossing arches, or on the crossing columns, as in the cathedrals of Rheims, Paris, London and Milan. From this ambition came that of erecting leaning towers which, even if they did not please the eye, stupefied the mind and terrified the spectator. And to decide which of these opposing aims is more glorious would be a problem worthy of an ingenious academician. It was from these Gothic examples that architects in the Roman line took courage and dared to raise cupolas above four piers, as in the cathedral of Florence and St. Peter's in Rome.

Guarini's imitations were never direct however. His was more a respect for the effects of Gothic structure rather than for its methods. Visual proof of the renewed interest in Gothic as opposed to simply classical architecture is provided by Juvarra, Guarini's successor in Turin. Juvarra's architecture, quite close in dramatic style to Guarini's, merges with fantasy in his *capriccios*, the wash drawings which bring to mind his own theatre designs. Folio 8 at Chatsworth House, Derbyshire, is essentially a fantasy, but it tells us a lot about the status of architecture: a fine Gothic church stands proud in the background of a sketch of classical ruins, it has no exact source and is more like the Gothic of Siena or Orvieto than that of Northern Europe. Although Guarini's *Architettura Civile* was not yet published it is tempting to assume that Juvarra had seen the manuscript since this is such a direct illustration of his ideas. Guarini's aim was not to be slavish, but to produce buildings to please reasonable judgement and judicious eye. Juvarra's second sketch, also a fantasy, is fascinating because it shows what is obviously a Baroque church but is artificially tall and vastly superior to the porticoed building portrayed in the foreground and to the right of the picture.

Guarini arrived in Turin in 1666 and it is no coincidence that his work flowered there. The seventeenth century had seen the rise of its rulers, the House of Savoy and the enlightened Duke Charles Emmanuel II transformed the face of Turin by his employment of Guarini and Juvarra and his enthusiasm for open architecture, which became so pronounced as to make it an identifiably

Piedmontese style. Guarini's two great works still standing in Turin, S. Lorenzo, the church for the Theatines, and the Capella Ss. Sindoni are works of hallucinatory engineering skill. The tiers of their domes are virtuoso constructions; their shapes interlock to create kaleidoscopic effects of light and pattern. The aerial structure is so eaten away with carving that all impression of weight is removed. This work has been compared to a Bach fugue; it has all the complexity but a much more dramatic effect. The centralised unexecuted church designs revealed by the *Architettura Civile* are of international importance since they were distributed in engraving form in 1686 before the publication of the whole work by Guarini's pupil, Bernardo Vittone, in 1737. These designs were for quite small churches and are in some ways more enjoyable because they are easier to understand. It is an immensely learned work and has a life and status of its own even though it is impossible for most people to follow the mathematics.

The design for S. Filippo in Casale, Monferrato is developed over an infinitely extended grid of pulsating cells, circular and square, with internally convex sides. Within this grid is a circle over which hangs the dome, yet this is integrated with its four surrounding cells. In it we can also see the curved window shapes of Guarini's invention emphasising the curves within the church which could be seen at Ste. Anne-la-Royale in Paris. The distinctive feature, however, of S. Filippo and S. Gaetano in Vicenza is the increased space of the lower storey created by using Gothic bundle piers to support the top storey, instead of either heavy pillars or solid piers. The dome of S. Gaetano is conventional and Mansardesque; it was due to have been covered with illusionistic frescoes, a sign that the superb ceiling painting that was to take over from decorative architecture in the Baroque of central Europe was beginning to be preferred over the miracle domes of S. Lorenzo.

S. Gaetano in Nizza (*c*.1670) would have been quite a small building on a pentagonal plan. It shows, surprisingly, a desire for simplification; it is still a very sophisticated interplay of straight and curved shapes but these are smoothly integrated and the exterior is clean and simple. As at S. Filippo, one would have entered the church through a pier which rises directly into the ribs supporting the upper storey. A tantalizing move towards comprehensibility emerges in this drawing which is not to be seen in any existing building by Guarini.

Through Guarini the open style became something of an obsession with the Dukes of Savoy and a style of Baroque was created which was to find another master in eighteenth-century Piedmont in Bernardo Vittone. It is, debatably, the most exciting expression of Baroque, if sometimes a problematic one. Borromini and Guarini, as distinct from Bernini and the Baroque architects of France, perfected an architectural form which was itself expressive and which broke down the barriers between painting and the decorative arts and architecture.

TEMPLI·IESV·ROMAE·PARS·ANTERIOR
IACOBO·VIGNOLA·ARCHITECTO·INVENTORE

Questa facciata nõ fu messa in opera per la morte del architetto.

Palmi Venginti Romani

Facciata de' Giesu come al presente si troua fatta da Iacomo della Porta.

45 Engraving by Mario Cartaro of Giacomo
Barozzi da Vignola's façade for the Gesù,
Rome.

46 Façade of the Gesù as executed by Giacomo
della Porta, engraving by Villamena.

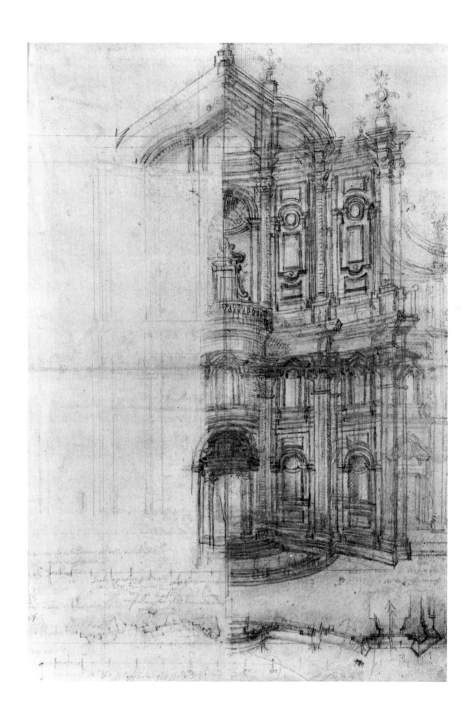

47 Borromini's superb sketch for the Oratorio
of S. Filippo Neri, Rome.

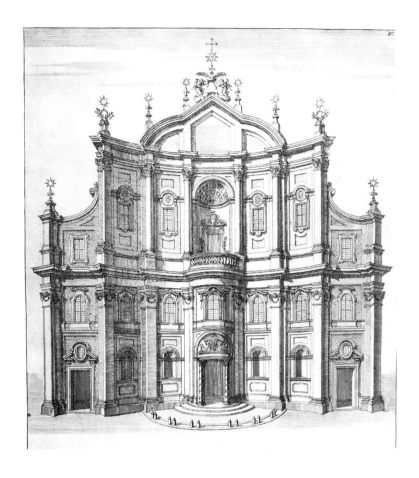

48 The opposing S-shaped curves of S.
   Filippo's façade enhanced by stone facing
   and symbolic decoration. This design was
   rejected by the Oratorians as being too
   grand.

49 The more economical design for S. Filippo
   as accepted and executed.

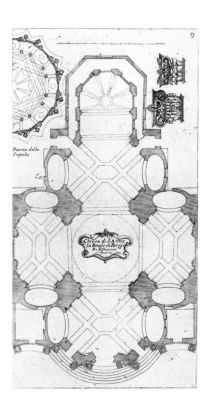

50 Profile of the lantern of S. Ivo alla Sapienza showing the sculptural symbolism which was so admired by Piedmontese architects such as Guarini and Vittone.

51 Engraving from Guarini's *Architettura Civile* of Ste. Anne-la-Royale, Paris, which was destroyed in 1823. The open stonework of the dome was to become a distinctive feature of his style.

52 Plan of Ste. Anne-la-Royale showing the sophistication of Guarini's geometry – especially in the detail of the dome.

53 Juvarra's capriccio of classical Rome
showing a splendid fantastical Gothic
church in the background.

54 Another capriccio by Juvarra, this time
showing a giant Baroque church which is
made to appear much grander than the
classical buildings in the foreground.

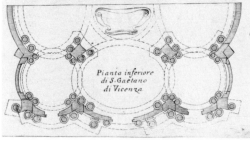

55 A design for S. Filippo in Casale, one of a
series of unexecuted centralised church
designs published in the *Architettura Civile*.
Its design is based on a series of interlocking
cells.

56 S. Gaetano di Vicenza – illusionistic
painting was planned to replace Guarini's
early ornate stonework.

57 Although more simple than some of his
proposed designs, this section of Guarini's
S. Gaetano in Nizza is still bizarre and
characteristically Piedmontese.

5. SIR CHRISTOPHER WREN AND ST. PAUL'S

*O*ld St. Paul's Cathedral, London, was the longest church in medieval Britain; it was also one of the most vulnerable. Suffering constantly from the filthy air of the city, it was struck by lightning in 1561 and lost the splendid wood and lead central spire that had dominated the London skyline. Then followed a period when all church buildings were neglected and when ruined monasteries, with hovels built within their damaged walls, gave the city an aura of decay. Churches which had escaped deliberate destruction at the Reformation were ignored. The stonework of St. Paul's was left to crumble and no concerted effort was made to restore the spire.

In the seventeenth century more attention was paid to the church. In 1608 Inigo Jones designed a domed finial to complete the truncated central tower. It was an uncertain, ogival, domed design, reflecting the discomfort felt by Jones in trying to blend his enthusiasm for things classical with an irrepressibly Gothic church. It was as well that this remained merely a study, being, in the words of Sir John Summerson 'obviously the work of somebody who had little to do with architecture and nothing with building'. At this time Jones was celebrated for his court masques rather than for more substantial works of architecture: but then this was before his most important visit to Italy in 1613-1614, when he, in the company of the Earl of Arundel, visited Milan, Padua, Siena, Florence, Bologna and Vicenza. They wintered in Rome, then departed for Naples, Venice, Vicenza again, Genoa and Turin, before returning to England via Paris. Jones's most important momento of this visit was his copy of Andrea Palladio's *Quattro Libri*, in which he wrote his own observations on Palladio's designs and on other classical buildings. His experience of classical architecture at first hand put him in a position unrivalled by his colleagues, manifested most strikingly at the Queen's House, Greenwich and the Banqueting House, Whitehall. His work on Old St. Paul's, since it was restorative, gave him less of a free hand, but one addition to that church was of unquestioned grandeur: this was the great Corinthian portico, larger than any other north of the Alps. With columns several storeys high, it was an opportunity for Jones to show off his experience of classical form. Other additions to the body of the church, the removal of the Norman windows of the nave and their replacement by mild classical ones were less majestic.

The ravages of time and Jones's additions left the cathedral an awkward stylistic hybrid: a sober, classically dressed nave, preceded by an exuberant portico; a damaged central tower, and a geometrical Gothic choir, the most magnificent feature of which was a rose window 60 feet across. It could not be described as a successful blend but it was a necessary one, given the dilapidation of the structure, and it is likely that the entire cathedral would have been enveloped in classical detail had fate not intervened.

The next stage, after Jones's works on the church, was to have been the restoration of the tower, which by the 1660s was giving serious cause for concern. Sir Christopher Wren, recently returned from a trip to France where he had met Bernini, reported on its structure. Wren did not propose that 'anything of Meer Beauty' be added, but where the vaults had distorted the columns, he considered that they should be rebuilt in 'a good Roman manner', in contrast to the despised 'rudeness' of the Gothic style.

Since the most dangerous part of the church was the crossing, Wren put forward the idea of a 'Dome or rotunda with a cupola'. This he intended to have built round the remnants of the old tower, for two reasons: one, to avoid excessive scaffolding, and, more beguilingly, 'partly because the expectations of persons is to be kept up (for many unbelievers would bewail the loss of Old St. Paul's steeple and despond if they did not see a hopeful successor rise in its stead)'.

This design was evidently indebted to Lemercier's church of the Sorbonne in Paris, which had moved Wren deeply. From this church Wren took the idea, one that remained a constant through all his plans, of an inner masonry dome with a taller outer timber one covered with lead. He was concerned that the inner dome should not seem too tall while the outer one should rise over the city. The outer treatment of the dome was simple and elegant, but terminated in an elongated open metalwork cone of questionable beauty. This would, however, have given the requisite degree of height to the church.

The Great Fire of September 1666 made these drawings irrelevant, but they do show how Wren's experience of French classical architecture influenced his thought. Immediately after the Fire, there was much discussion as to what to do with St. Paul's: though the body of the church was in ruins its services still had to carry on. A rapid survey by Wren revealed that the least damaged part of the building was the western end of the nave. Early in 1668 work began on a temporary choir in this part of the church, but almost immediately more parts of the structure collapsed. Dean Sancroft wrote to Wren to ask to see his pre-Fire drawings again. Wren's response was to urge the Dean to think of 'a new fabrick upon new foundations, artificiall, durable and beautifull, but less massive' than the old. He soon also reported on more falls of masonry, which were likely to endanger the tower.

In July of that year the vital decision was made to commence demolition of Old St. Paul's, which provided the great opportunity to build a new cathedral, a move encouraged by Sancroft's comment that the size of the new church should not be restricted by the amount of money that could be anticipated.

The first design provoked by the admission that an entirely new church was needed was available by autumn 1669. Our knowledge of this is based on the partial fragment of a model still surviving, comments by Sir Roger Pratt and a sketchy drawing. Piece these together and we have a cathedral with a barrel-vaulted nave and a domed vestibule to its west, 60 feet in diameter; added to the latter were three 'porticoes' which were scorned by Pratt.

Pratt was not the only one to criticise the scheme: *Parentalia*, the copious memoir of Wren written by his son, stated that the First Model lacked the importance of 'the old Gothick Form of Cathedral Churches' and that it was not stately enough. The first was an understandable comment. We cannot properly reconstruct the exterior of this church; irritatingly, we have very little idea of the sort of dome intended, but it can be assumed that at around 200 feet long the church was insufficiently impressive. Old St. Paul's, after all, was at least 600 feet long; Westminster Abbey, the largest surviving church in London was 500; the cathedrals at Winchester, Ely, Canterbury, York and Durham were of equal size. The scale of Wren's new church compared very unfavourably with these buildings. By 'old Gothick form', Wren's critics had in mind the plan of these churches, long and cruciform. Wren's church did not offer that, either. Rather than overwhelming its critics with grandeur, it was at once too unexpected, too small in stature and too original in form.

The criticism that Wren's design lacked grandeur was not entirely unwelcome. 'After this, in order to find what might satisfy the World, the Surveyor drew several sketches merely for Discourse-sake, and observing the Generality were for Grandeur, he endeavour'd to gratify the Taste of the Connoisseurs and Criticks, conformable to the best Stile of the Greek and Roman architecture.' The resultant design was almost certainly that known as the Greek Cross Design. This was of four equal arms linked by curving exterior walls; three out of the four sides were adorned by porticos; the fourth, being the choir, did not need an entrance. This was both an ambitious and an imposing church. The sophisticated curving walls brought to mind the various proposals, unexecuted and otherwise, for St. Peter's Rome: the dome, too, immediately reminded its discerning observers of continental antecedents. Perhaps more important was its innovative (for England) display of centralised planning. The chapter in this book on St. Peter's has examined the origin and development of this type of church: here Wren put forward a design for the first centralised church in England with any hope of execution. It lacked a close and obvious relationship with Gothic antecedents, but it did have the desired degree of magnificence, and Wren was instructed to elaborate on these designs in the form of a model. According to *Parentalia*, 'Persons of Distinction, Skilled in Antiquity and Architecture' requested that 'a very curious large Model in Wood' be made. The result was the Great Model made in 1673-74. In overall plan this was the Greek Cross church with the addition at the west end of a smaller dome over a portico. The model, 30 feet long, which still exists in the crypt of St. Paul's cathedral, was presented on a

trestle to Charles II. Sir Robert Hooke, diarist and commissioner for rebuilding London, saw it when it still needed paint on its interior: nonetheless it gave an impressive idea to all those filing below it of the classical centralised massing that Wren intended.

Although externally the Great Model had a western emphasis, with its smaller dome echoing the main one, internally it was as determinedly centralised as the Greek Cross plan. It was therefore as hard to accept as the Greek Cross design: the Chapter and the clergy in general felt that it was 'not enough of a cathedral fashion'. It was same complaint as before – traditionally an English church still had to have a strong longitudinal emphasis with nave, crossing and choir.

Having proceeded as far as the beautiful, expensive and, Wren hoped, persuasive model only to have it rejected, the architect turned to a different type of church having 'resolved to make no more Models or publickly expose his Drawings, which (as he had found by Experience) did but lose Time and subjected his Business many Times to incompetent Judges'. His next design for St. Paul's was undeniably long and cruciform, with a lengthy nave of six bays, a shorter but still noticeable choir, and prominent transepts. The elevation of the church was in marked contrast to Wren's earlier churches. Instead of the usual central unity supplied by the overwhelming presence of the domed central space, here was a long, low church, with a central dome, but a dome oppressed, depressed in a literal sense, by a steeple rising in stages, not unlike that subsequently erected for St. Bride's, Fleet Street. The dome immediately under this spire rested on a drum above a very flattened saucer-like dome.

Visually it was not a success. Indeed the whole church was very much a backwards step, both in planning and ornament. With its round-headed windows under square surrounds, and flat pilasters topped by low pinnacles, it bore a noticeable resemblance to the modified nave of Old St. Paul's after Inigo Jones's restoration. The spire was an echo, albeit a strident one, of the lost spire of Old St. Paul's. It is hard to believe that Wren, who so admired Bernini and Parisian architecture could feel entirely happy with such a church; it was very much a compromise, but one which worked for his clients. This scheme became known as the Warrant Design because attached to it was a royal warrant dated 14th May 1675; the warrant authorised the immediate commencement of the building, and by mid-June contracts with the masons had been signed. More than any previous Wren design, the Warrant Design had an air of the medieval about it. Particularly intriguing was its relationship to Ely Cathedral, a church where Wren's uncle was bishop. The octagonal central space of St. Paul's to which the nave and aisles had direct access, was particularly redolent of that Fenland cathedral.

PLATE VI The Warrant design, had it been built, would have provided London with an eye-catching curiosity – a spire of unquestionable height but questionable taste. It was never built because Wren's high esteem in the eyes of the King allowed continued creative revisions of the scheme.

The most immediate and important revision was to replace the spire with a more conventional dome, of hemispherical shape. This, the penultimate design, was reconstructed by Sir John Summerson from fragmentary drawings. Its drawback was a lack of height, only 200 feet high it would still have risen above seventeenth-century London, but greater height was admired. Wren knew, and had been surveyor to, Salisbury Cathedral: at 404 feet, the spire there was entirely more visible. In size, the penultimate design for St. Paul's was much smaller than the 300 feet dome of the rejected Great Model. His problem, if he wished such height now, was how to impose it on his longitudinal church. Whereas the Great Model was almost a plinth for a massive dome, with the Warrant Design the balance was reversed; the dome being subservient to the main body of the building.

Wren found an ingenious solution: he designed blank screen walls to the upper part of the church, giving the erroneous but appealing impression that his newly enlarged dome was supported on a great mass of masonry. They also hid the flying buttresses that Wren now intended as support for the vault. In Wren's finely executed drawing for this variant, dated 1675, we have a cathedral very close to that which was finally built: the subtlety of the relationship of the round porches to the transepts, the screen walls, the balancing of the dome by the smaller western towers. Only in details was this a different church: the surface treatment of the dome, the elevation of the west towers. Here the towers are tiny replicas of the central dome as built. The surface of the main dome too changed: in the 1675 drawing it is heavily panelled with squares containing occuli but these round windows were never executed. Otherwise, we here have the cathedral as built. To achieve this happy conclusion Wren had moved from the advocation of a dome preceded solely by a nave (the First Model), a dome on four equal arms (the Greek Cross), a centralised domed church with a narthex (the Great Model) and a long domed church unhappily pierced by a spire (the Warrant Design) to the final scheme of a longitudinal church oversailed by a dome balanced by two western towers. These changes were the results of the pressure of the patron: nonetheless the final result must have satisfied the architect.

58 Sir Christopher Wren, portrait by Kneller, showing the architect resting his arm on a ground plan of St. Paul's Cathedral.

59 Old St. Paul's as Wren intended it in 1666. The dome to replace the weakened medieval central tower ends in a peculiar open metalwork spire that has been criticised as 'an architectural pineapple'. Wren also intended to dress the Romanesque nave (on the left) with classical ornament, but left the Geometrical choir unaltered.

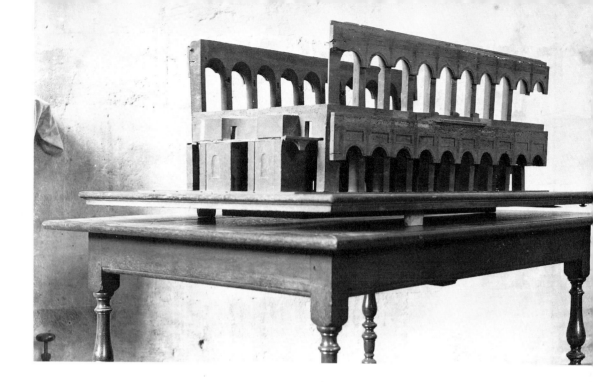

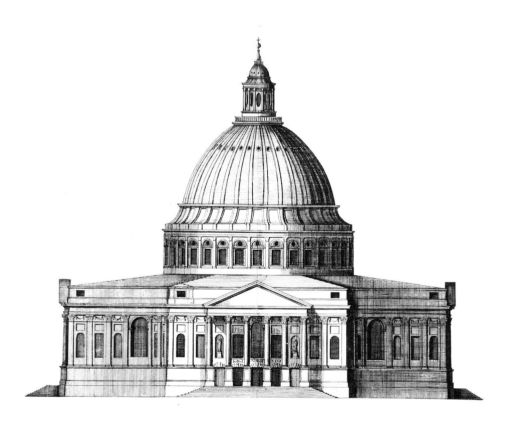

60 Surviving fragment of Wren's first design for St. Paul's which was soundly criticised for its lack of grandeur.

61 The Greek Cross design. All four arms, nave, transepts and choir were of equal length, a revolutionary piece of planning that proved too much for Wren's more conservative patrons.

62 The Great Model from the north-east, the choir indicated by the small, eastern apse.

63 The Great Model from the west. The model which survives in the crypt of St. Paul's, was a design closely related to the Greek Cross Design, with the addition of a domed narthex at the west and a spectacular portico.

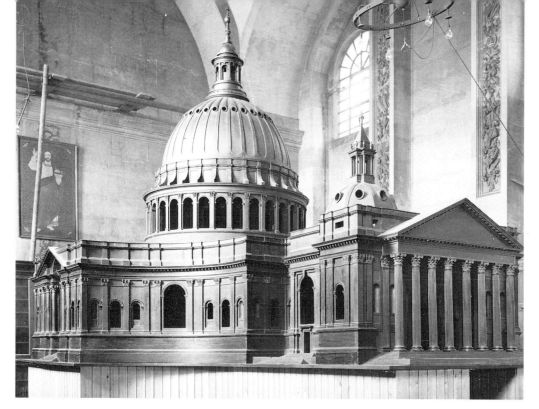

64 The Great Model from the north. When
presented to Charles II, it was raised on a
trestle so that the King and others could
walk under it and examine the interior.

65 The Great Model opened, the east end at
the bottom of the page. Its centralised
planning is obvious. The narthex at the west
end in no way impinges on the plan
inherited from the Greek Cross Design.

66 Inside the Great Model. The enormous
space under the dome is well conveyed, as is
the detail of the interior ornament. Wren's
frustration at the final rejection of the
scheme is understandable.

67 The Warrant Design: after the rejection of the Great Model, Wren gave in to conservative pressure to produce a design with a long nave. This was the result.

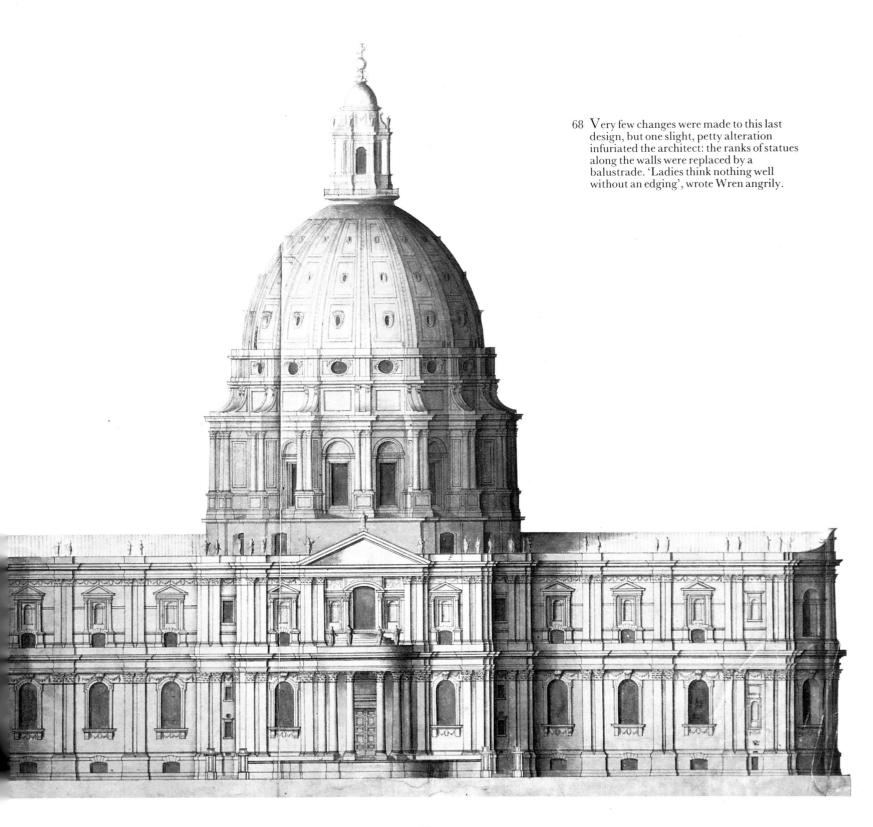

68 Very few changes were made to this last design, but one slight, petty alteration infuriated the architect: the ranks of statues along the walls were replaced by a balustrade. 'Ladies think nothing well without an edging', wrote Wren angrily.

6. RESTRAINT AND DISPLAY IN THE EIGHTEENTH CENTURY

*T*he eighteenth century was not the era of the church; certainly not in Britain. No opportunity for a new cathedral like St. Paul's presented itself; no disaster created a need for a city full of classical churches. It was the age of the secular building: architects who published collections of their designs devoted their energies to country houses, imaginary royal palaces and the occasional public building. Churches were in the minority.

PLATE VII

Nonetheless it would be wrong to assume that church building entirely ceased. Enough were erected for Marcus Whiffen to write his charming study of Stuart and Georgian churches outside London, and several commissions engaged the talents of designers in a way wholly worthy of our attention. James Gibbs not only gave us St. Martin's-in-the-Fields as it is now, but a series of alternatives all presented in his *A Book of Architecture, containing Designs of Buildings and Ornaments* MD CCXXVIII. The text of Gibbs's dedication is important to our understanding of the influences on his architecture:

> To his grace John, Duke of Argyll and Greenwich &c one of his Majesty's most Honourable Privy Council, Colonel of the Queen's own Royal Regiment of Horse, General of the Foot, Master General of the Ordnance, and Knight of the most Noble Order of the Garter . . The early encouragement I received from Your Grace, in my profession upon my return from Italy, and the Honour of your protection ever since, give your name a just title to all my productions in this kind . . . As several of the design here exhibited have had Your Grace's Approbation; so your patronage will be sufficient recommendation to the whole work.
>
> It is a particular pleasure to me that this Publication gives me an opportunity to declare the real sentiments of gratitude and respect with which I am, My Lord, Your Grace's Most Dutiful and most Obliged humble servant, James Gibbs.'

Apart from the determinedly obliging tone, this dedication is of interest because it pinpoints Gibbs's visit to Italy which made him unusual among his contemporaries. As a Scottish catholic, he was able to enjoy the company of contemporary architects working there with Carlo Fontana, the seventeenth-century Roman architect, and learning at first hand of current use of motifs. Whole buildings and their decorative lesser parts were presented in Gibbs's book which bear witness to his Italian experience, but it was an experience muted by the strictures of that Palladianism then dominant in England. Gibbs was determined to reach the appropriate market, and that market was not the churchman, eagerly awaiting new ideas on church decoration, but his secular counterpart, the country gentleman:

> What is here presented to the Publick was undertaken at the instance of several persons of quality and others . . . They were of the opinion that such a work as this would be of use to such gentlemen as might be concerned in Building, especially in the remote parts of the Country, where little or no assistance for designs can be procured. Such may be furnished with Draughts of useful and convenient Buildings and proper ornaments; which may be executed by any workman who understands lines.

Gibbs warned of the dangers in allowing workman a free hand:

> Some, for want of better Helps, have unfortunately put into the hands of common workmen, the management of Buildings of considerable expence; which when finished they have had the mortification to find condemned by persons of Tast, to that degree that sometimes they have been pull'd down, at least alter'd at a greater charge than would have procur'd better advice from an able Artist; or if they have stood, they have remained lasting Monuments of the Ignorance or Parsimoniousness of the Owners, or (it maybe) of a wrong-judged Profuseness
>
> In order to prevent the Abuses and Absurdities above hinted at, I have taken the utmost care that these designs should be done in the best Tast I could form upon the Instructions of the greatest masters in Italy, as well as my own observations upon the antient Buildings there, during many years application to these studies: For a cursory View of those August remains can no more qualify the Spectator or Admirer, than the Air of the Country can inspire him with the knowledge of Architecture.'

This emphasis was on taste and on conformity applied to country houses, not to churches. But it is instructive to look at his comments on St Martin-in-the-Fields. That church resulted not from a spontaneous enthusiasm for a new church, but from the delapidation of a medieval predecessor:

> being decayed and in danger of falling, the Parishioners obtain'd an Act of Parliament for Rebuilding it at their own charges. The Commissioners appointed therein were pleased to make a choice of me for Surveyor of that work; and several Plans of different forms being prepar'd and laid before them, they fix'd upon the following, as most proper for that site. There were two designs made for a round church, which were approved by the commissioners, but were laid aside upon account of the

expensiveness of executing them; tho' they were more capacious and convenient than what they pitch'd upon: I have inserted them likewise in this book. The commissioners having signed the Plan agreed on, gave me orders to begin the work; and everything being ready for laying the Foundation, His Majesty was pleased to direct the Right Reverend the Bishop of Salisbury, then Lord Almoner, attended by Sir Thomas Hewyt, then Surveyor General, to lay the first stone of the Fabrick.

This ceremony being over, I proceeded with the Building, and finished it in five years; which, notwithstanding the great Economy of the Commissioners, cost the parish upwards of 32,000 Pounds. I have given here seven plates of this Church.

Gibbs's rejected and costly design was extremely adventurous for England and had definite Italian prototypes. The plan derived from a similar one in Andrea Pozzo's book on perspective, which had appeared in an English edition in 1707. The fact that Gibbs so diligently recorded the design meant that it was available to influence the occasional provincial scheme. Sir John Summerson has pointed out the echoes of its plan at St. Paul's, Liverpool by T. Lightoller 1765-69 and St. Chad's Shrewsbury by George Stuart 1790-92. All were intriguing – St. Chad's especially has an airy grace about it, but the Gibbs prototype had the edge as regards ingenuity. More importantly, it went on to influence Sir William Chambers when he designed his unrealised parish church for Marylebone, fifty years after Gibbs's abortive round church. Marylebone, amongst the most rapidly growing areas of eighteenth-century London, required an appropriate parish church. Chambers initially wrote to the Reverend John Harley on the subject of two designs, one domed, the other with a spire. He was refreshingly candid:

> I have estimated the different designs for Marylebone church and find that the Dome will exceed the sum you propose laying out quite considerably & the solidity of the work requires so many Precautions which affect the convenience of the building that I do not think the Dome so proper a design as the other.

The circumstances of the church were not the most auspicious. The sponsors of the project were vacillating in their attempts to choose a site, while funding was extremely precarious. It was perhaps foolhardy of them to choose then the most costly domed variant, and the predictable delays and confusions so frequently associated with such ventures immediately beset all concerned. Chambers's wrath at the unsatisfactory proceedings was to be expected:

> I have already made five if not six different designs, some of them very considerable ones. I have also made several estimates of this building & in the whole been at a Good deal of Expense and had a great deal of trouble.

E Indeed he had: his elevations were executed with finesse and his longitudinal section was as delicately and seductively coloured as his more renowned work for York House in Pall Mall, for the Duke of York. In both designs the watercolour work, especially on the domes, is first class. The galleried interior shows subtle use of shadow and perspective. An attractive and persuasive touch was Chambers's insertion of a tiny altar complete with communion goblet, draped in folds of cloth. Unlike many domed churches, such as St. Paul's Cathedral, Chambers's St. Marylebone had a dome which looked almost the same from the outside as from the inside. It was a supreme example of architectural chasteness, allied to the excitement that a dome always brings to a church. Less thrilling for Chambers was the parsimonious sum of £100 which his patrons offered him for his prodigious amount of work. He had provided a finely worked elevation for the imposing façade: the dome rose determinedly behind a large unadorned pediment, the severity of the upper part softened by swags of carved foliage between its small square windows. The plan he submitted exploited to the full the potential of the circular. All in all, Chambers was shabbily treated by his would-be patrons, and can have drawn little comfort from the fact that a decidedly inferior church was eventually built. It was especially galling that the history of this, the most important church in London for almost sixty years, should end so unsatisfactorily.

Chambers was an adamant Palladian. It would be safe to assume that Colen Campbell, arch exponent of the form in his vastly influential *Vitruvius Britannicus*, would have approved his efforts. Campbell was less keen on its prototype by Gibbs, an architect whom he had previously criticised. Campbell himself designed a church on a monumental scale, one which he put in ambitious context by prefacing it with the designs for St. Paul's Cathedral and St. Peter's Rome. His own scheme for Lincoln's Inn Fields was proposed with optimism and showed a very derivative domed design echoing loudly that of St. Peter's.

What both Campbell and Chambers had avoided when possible was the spire. The dome not the spire was the great feature of a classical church. There were, after all, tainted associations for spires. Gibbs had said of them:

> Steeples indeed are of a Gothic Extraction, but they have their beauties, when their parts are well disposed and when the plans of the several Degrees and Orders of which they are composed gradually diminish and pass from one form to another without confusion, and when every part has the appearance of a proper bearing.

Like Nicholas Hawksmoor, Gibbs felt that the spire, carefully managed, had its uses. It was important to avoid Gothic overtones: In 1578 Palladio himself had said that Gothic 'was confusion, not architecture' and it would have taken a courageous architect to gainsay that dictator of taste in eighteenth-century England. Hawksmoor had surveyed Beverley Minster in Yorkshire and had published comparatively detailed and accurate engravings based on his measurements. He was celebrated for his handling of All Souls College, Oxford, and for his comments on the merits of the fifteenth-century original buildings, which he contrasted with the 'perishable fantastical Trash' that his contemporaries sometimes erected. It is questionable whether Hawksmoor was consciously imitating church towers of the Middle Ages when designing his churches in east London for the Fifty New Churches Act, but he did make extensive use of the spire for Christ Church, Spitalfields which was almost entirely medieval in appearance. Hawksmoor was also responsible for an unexecuted design which combined both an enthusiasm for classical forms, carefully manipulated, with an impression of verticality that echoed the nature of the commission, for this was his campanile for King's College, Cambridge. Hawksmoor's plan for the college in its most extensive form involved the destruction of all the medieval work other than the great chapel with its large Perpendicular windows and its vertical Perpendicular pinnacles. A medieval campanile had been intended at one point, but Hawksmoor did not follow that dictate. Instead his campanile, plain on its lower storeys, more articulated with classical form towards the top, was uncompromisingly classical yet consistent with the need for a vertical emphasis in the college, to compliment the large Perpendicular chapel. Had it been built, Hawksmoor's campanile would have echoed the verticality, the slenderness of the chapel, without being in any way compromised by its architectural style; a harmony of differences would have been achieved.

The close of the eighteenth century and the opening of the nineteenth century brought perhaps one of the more important opportunities for church building in England. Unlike a hundred years previously there was no threat of popery, there was no fear of Roman interference in English society. But amongst the outer suburbs of London and perhaps also in the industrial towns of the North and Midlands, the Non-Conformist churches were gaining large numbers of new converts. And even more alarming to churchgoers of every creed was the rising popularity of out-and-out atheism. A writer in the *Quarterly Review* in 1820 discussed this situation:

> The populous are told in plain terms that religion is a mere juggle between priests and kings, for the purpose of keeping them in subjection; that men are like the beasts that perish; and that as they have no other world to look for, they are fools if they refrain from any gratification which this can give them, also for any prejudice to stand in the way of their interests and their inclination.

This was a wholly alarming state of affairs to the Church and to the Establishment, and to combat this, large new churches were called for. The result was the Church Building Act of 1818 in which new churches were to be constructed in newly expanded urban areas such as Liverpool as well as in London. These were mainly large galleried classical churches. Their importance in architectural history is that architects now chose, with happy indiscretion, from a number of styles. Admittedly some of the more spectacular churches such as that eventually built in Marylebone, and others in London, are mainly in the classical style, often the Doric, but Gothic versions were seen nonetheless as just as feasible.

This is nowhere more evocatively illustrated than in some schemes by Sir John Soane, illustrated by J.M. Gandy. Preserved PLAT in Sir John Soane's Museum in Lincoln's Inn Fields, these designs show not only an interest in a variety of architectural styles, but also the manipulative powers of the perspectivist executing an architect's basic scheme. Most brilliant of all, in both respects, is the panorama of a hillside of potential churches, some executed but many not, illustrated on the cover of this book. Soane's dramatic use of light and shade, and his evocative use of colour create a vision of an ecclesiastical city. The Gothic unexecuted churches from this scheme are particularly attenuated, and it is instructive to compare a Gothic scheme with a classical one from this era. In planning terms they are very similar – it is only in the execution of their ornament that they differ.

Here then we have a reversal of the eighteenth-century practice, instead of rejecting the concept of a Gothic church, as Campbell and his Palladian colleagues had done early in the century, architects now felt that Gothic had been rehabilitated. Through the later eighteenth century, Gothic had been used as a flippant, delicate, enjoyable style, best suited to lodges, gazebos, garden building generally, and other small, insignificant buildings which were designed for pleasure and delightful display rather than for any serious purpose. By 1818 the Gothic style had become more acceptable for major churches. This is not to deny that Gothic churches had been built throughout the eighteenth century, especially in the provinces, but often they were on a small scale, and certainly not the result of major architects choosing the style. By 1818 we are heading towards the age of eclecticism, the age where style was very much the choice of the architect, the age after all when the Egyptian style, the Indian or Hindoo style, so charmingly named, were all possibilities; although perhaps the latter would not have been considered suitable for a church, one could have a Romanesque church, a Gothic one, or an Italianate one. Any style of Christian architecture certainly seemed sensible and acceptable for architects practising in church buildings. This rehabilitation of styles other than the classical preceded the great nineteenth-century bias towards the Gothic, but at the time of the Commissioner's churches, Soane's hillside of churches, shows more than any other scheme the move from pure classicism to eclecticism, a move from rigorously severe building to the sort of perspective which invites an emotive response.

69 J. M. Williams's portrait of James Gibbs, the Scottish Catholic architect who worked under Fontana in Rome, designed St. Martin's-in-the-Fields and who published one of the most influential of all eighteenth-century books on architecture.

70 East-west section through the round design for St. Martin's-in-the-Fields, which was rejected because it was too costly.

71 St. Martin's-in-the-Fields. Gibbs's most original design with a round nave, view from the west.

72 West elevation of one of Sir William Chambers's unexecuted designs for St. Marylebone Church, London.

73 Ground plan of a Chambers's design for St. Marylebone.

74 The plan of Campbell's church reveals his debt to those who evolved the centrally planned church in Italy.

75 Colen Campbell's 'Design of my Invention for a Church in Lincoln's Inn Fields', a huge domed church with obvious debts to St. Peter's. Campbell published it in *Vitruvius Britannicus*.

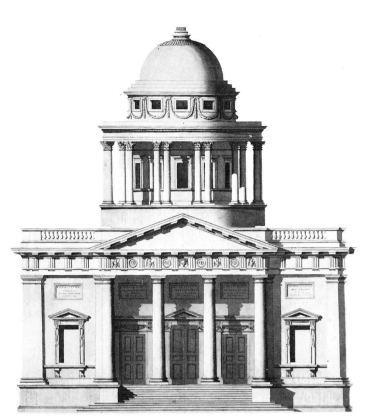

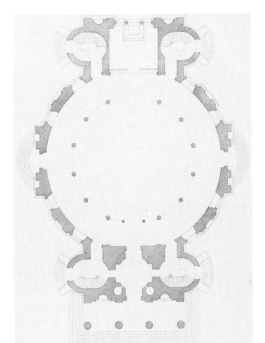

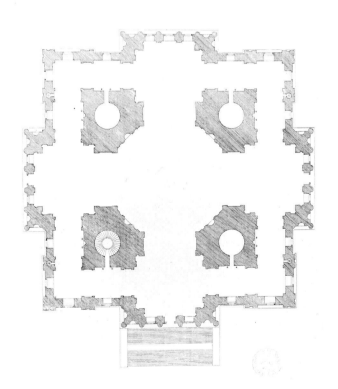

76 Gibbs's *Book of Architecture* contained
numerous examples of spires that were
never built: these were influential in the
provinces but more importantly, inspired
many churches in America.

77 Another set of spires from Gibbs's *Book of Architecture*.

78 Gibbs's spires, from his *Book of Architecture*.

79 Hawksmoor at his most audacious. King's
College, Cambridge would have had a
severe classical campanile to accompany its
chapel, had the architect's most sweeping
changes been instigated.

7. THE RETURN TO GOTHIC IN THE NINETEENTH CENTURY

*T*he intensity of church building activity in nineteenth-century Britain provided unprecedented opportunity for architects. It was a situation undreamt of at the beginning of the century. In 1845 *The Builder* carried in its pages a glowing review of 'The 25th Annual Report of the Commissioners for Building New Churches'. 'It appears that 343 churches have now been completed, and provision has therein been made for 402,259 persons, including 225,217 seats appropriated to the use of the poor. . . . There are 36 churches now in the course of building . . . plans for 23 churches have now been approved . . . Applications have been made to the Commissioners from 74 places. A most satisfactory result.'

By the 1830s the Established Church had realized the need to re-assert its influence after a period of some neglect in the eighteenth century. Spurred on by the challenge of the Evangelical Movement, the removal of restrictions on both Dissenters and Roman Catholics, and a fear, after the Napoleonic wars, that a godless population was a population ripe for revolution, the building programme had gathered momentum.

The question of architectural style was not at first one of great importance, apart from the implications of expense. In his *Recollections* Sir George Gilbert Scott, the most prolific of nineteenth-century architects, singled out Charles Barry's churches of the late 1820s as 'respectable and well-intentioned'. For the most part, a few pointed arches and insubstantial, vaguely Gothicising forms were assumed largely for cheapness sake. Scott wrote 'I hardly view those (years) which preceded 1830 (or even a later date) as belonging to the period of the (Gothic) revival at all'. Even his own churches of 1838-41 he condemned as 'as bad, or nearly so, as the rest', confessing 'Often . . . have I been wicked enough to wish my works burnt down again'. He expressed not only the pressures of time and economy, but admitted 'an utter want of appreciation of what a church should be'.

Awareness of church ritual and respect for the functions of ecclesiastical buildings were the crux of the matter. Scott quite simply said 'From this darkness the subject was suddenly opened out by Augustus Welby Pugin, and the Cambridge Camden Society'.

The subject of church design was opened out not only by practical example but by an enormous publication of theory. A.W.N. Pugin, who worked with Barry on the Houses of Parliament in the 1830s, was from 1835 a fervent convert to Roman Catholicism. He expounded his passionate theory of Gothic as the essential national and Christian style under such revealing titles as *The True Principles of Pointed or Christian Architecture* (1841) and *An Apology for the Revival of Christian Architecture in England* (1843). The Cambridge Camden Society were an Anglican group, sympathizing with the spiritual doctrines of the Oxford Tractarians. They promoted a 'correct' Gothic style as appropriate for ecclesiastical building in their journal *The Ecclesiologist*, published 1841-68. The classical style, with its 'pagan' associations, the focus on the pulpit, the galleried preaching-house, was out. Renewed consideration of the liturgy and spiritual purpose, the symbolism of the medieval cruciform plan, the holy significance of the chancel, were in. It was no longer sufficient to appropriate a few, cheaply rendered Gothic forms at random; sound archaeological knowledge was required.

PLATE X
PLATE XI

In Pugin's *True Principles* doctrine and style were inexorably harnessed for ecclesiastical building. He argued his subject from every angle – a nationalist argument: classical and Renaissance styles belong to Greece and Italy, Gothic to England – a practical argument: how well suited is Gothic to the English climate, a correctly pitched roof throwing off rain and snow. He argued for propriety 'regulated by function and purpose' of a small parish church or large cathedral. He argued for 'truth'. Further, he said that form should express the functions of each part, chancel, nave, porch and tower, with no need for classical symmetry, that materials should be crafted with care and honestly used, not disguised or simulated by paint and plaster. The open-wood roofs of old churches should be revived in place of the modern deceits of plaster ceilings; attention should be paid to the very last detail of church furniture and fittings. He called not for 'servile' imitation, but for the 'principles' and 'consistent spirit of ancient architects'.

The impact of the Revival theory was voiced by Scott in somewhat emotional terms. 'Pugin's articles (in the *Dublin Review*) excited me almost to fury, and I suddenly found myself like a person awakened from a long and feverish dream.' It sounds deceptively simple.

Thomas Rickman had, in 1819, already categorized Gothic in the three phases we still know: Early English, Decorated (also known as Middle Pointed) and the latest, Perpendicular. This was the form roughly referred to in most of the early Commissioner's churches, but seen by Pugin and the Cambridge Camden Society as a decline from the perfection of Middle Pointed. The appropriate use of one or other type provided fertile ground for argument, voiced in countless letters and articles sent to newspapers and journals of the day. What is more, many designs were drawn-up in every detail but never executed, or, at best, were radically altered because of financial constraints or a lack of accord between architect and patron or committee. Such was the fate of Pugin himself.

Pugin's designs of 1839 for the first Roman Catholic cathedral built in England since the Reformation, St. Chad's in Birmingham, suffered from essential economies. He managed to maintain a splendidly rich interior with dramatic exaggeration of the relation of height to breadth, while acceding to a plain brick exterior, with very little stone decoration, saying 'It must be readily admitted that to have sacrificed the internal splendour of the House of God for the sake of exterior display, would have been utterly departing from true Catholic Principles'.

With reference to St. George's Cathedral, Southwark, *The Builder* announced to its readers in June 1843 'This superb building now being erected by Mr. Welby Pugin, begins to assume a most imposing appearance'. It makes the point, in italics, that 'there will be no ornamental plasterwork whatever in this building, all the ornaments being carved either in stone or oak, without repetition of design'. Yet Pugin had been anything but a free agent. The committee had rejected his initial proposal of 1839, raising what he considered captious objections. With intense disappointment he withdrew from the whole scheme, only to be lured back by the bait of what *The Builder* described at its opening in 1848 as, 'the most important structure which the English Roman Catholics have built in modern times'. Pugin was to raise a large church on a constricted, triangular site, dictating a disproportionately long nave. In his first scheme, he responded with relish to the challenge, using a tall, richly decorated, centrally placed tower and massing constructional form and detail at the crossing. How successfully this would have overcome the problem of length, and avoided any hint of repetitive monotony. As it was, the tower and 'bulk' was placed at the west end, and for all Pugin's efforts, and *The Builder*'s 'imposing appearance', the St. George's compromise resulted in something like an overgrown parish church. In 1850, two years before his death, Pugin wrote defensively that it 'was spoilt by the very instructions laid down by the committee'.

If the nineteenth-century was an age of great architectural activity, it was also the great age of the architectural competition, and that, like any other, allowed for only one winner. In May, 1872, *The Builder* carried a heartfelt moral tale, *'The Story of a Competition'*.

The Story of a Competition

An architect sits in his office alone:
Tis night; work is over, the drawings are done:–
. . .
He scans them with pride – not unmix'd with dismay,
At the time and the money they've frittered away . . .'

The lure of an important competition was hard to resist, but

You'll imagine perhaps that of those who take part
In the judgement some few have a knowledge of art.
No such thing . . .

Whether the judges were qualified to perform their task or not was a frequent cause of complaint. The writer warns too of favouritism, which could circumvent the rules of anonymity. He might well have added that even the winner might not necessarily see his scheme built.

William Burges and Henry Clutton won the 1855-56 international competition for a thirteenth-century Gothic style cathedral at Lille, and Burges won that for the English Crimea Memorial Church at Constantinople, immediately afterwards. Neither design was built.

Both competitions inspired great interest in England, *The Builder* printed an especially intriguing French appreciation of Lille, by the journalist Cauvin. 'The English architects will be glad to see the unbiased criticism of an intelligent foreign writer on a subject to all of great interest', said *The Builder*'s introduction while Cauvin himself was generous:

> We heartily approve of the mode adopted at Lille, which, by inviting to the contest the architects of every country, has performed an act truly *catholic* in the real sense of the word, so that the presence of England, of Germany, of Belgium, at this peaceful battle, has shown what was the state of the art in these different countries. In France the artists, like the soldiers, do not see in a defeat anything more than a signal for fresh exertions, and as giving an opportunity for a glorious revenge . . .

> Be that as it may, the concursus at Lille was most brilliant. There were forty-one competitors. Of this number, fifteen belonged to France, fourteen to England, and one to Scotland: Rhenish Prussia sent three; the Grand Duchy of Baden, two; Austria, one; Hanover, one; and Silesia, one; making in all eight for Germany. It is now seen that, in the number of competitors, France and England were equal and completely rivals, the contest between whom was hot and warmly discussed. England obtained two prizes, the first and second . . . it is rather singular, we must admit, that a Catholic country such as France is, should yield the palm, at a solemn concursus, to a Protestant country, and that, too, for the object of creating a cathedral.

But Cauvin went on to praise English architecture:

> By little and little the liking has gone down for the uncouth architecture of columns, which has infested London and England with so many awkward and clumsy buildings; and the new school swears, by the climate of Great Britain, that it will, with predilection, with ardour, study the forms of the national architecture during the Middle Ages . . .

> Under the fertilizing influence of such encouragement, numbers of religious edifices have been erected; and all have seen rising up on the banks of the Thames, as a testimonial of the living power and force of the renovating movement, the prodigious monument, the Houses of Parliament, having an appearance fairy-like, and at the same time grand in the extreme.

Patriotic pride was felt at the result of Lille, where, from 41 entries, George Edmund Street ran a close second to Burges, and six other Englishmen were medallists or were commended including R.B. Pullan. Intense disappointment was voiced when the jury's decision was rejected, and a young, unsuccessful competitor, a local man, was called on to execute a conglomerate scheme incorporating shadows of Burges's and Street's designs. *The Ecclesiologist* blamed French national pride, a 'clique' and 'backstairs'. By August, 1856, *The Builder* tersely said, 'Our countrymen have closed the correspondence'.

For Constantinople, Burges and Street again took first and second prizes, but between 1856 and 1863 Burges was called on several times to reduce his scheme, and Turkish inflation contributed to his difficulties. His first plan of a nave with six bays was reduced to five, then four, three and two. He agreed to lose the flying buttresses of the ambulatory, allowed for cheaper methods of construction, sacrificed the polychromatic impact of his first design, and ended with something akin to monochrome, Early French Gothic. After all this, it was a revised design by Street that was built.

The schemes for both competitions reflected not only individual attitudes and characteristics of design, but a general shift of 'Gothic taste' from Pugin's and the Cambridge Camden Society's preference for Middle Pointed. The Cambridge Camden Society, known as the Ecclesiological Society from 1845, itself changed position in the 1850s and 1860s. It successively promoted a greater emphasis on the wall-surface, on the structural use of coloured materials, on horizontality, or a 'primitive', 'muscular' simplicity and then on a heavy massiveness of effect. According to Scott, the influence of the Ecclesiologists was almost tyrannical, and so, their acceptance of new modes significant.

The Ecclesiologist at first pronounced Burges's work for Lille 'rather austerely conceived' having 'ungainly and under-developed forms'. While admiring its grandiose effect 'one regrets constantly that some of the rudeness and eccentricity of a too early style have not been abandoned'. It preferred Street's design, which was stylistically later in detail and, it judged, more original in concept. Of Pullan, one of the silver-medallists, it admired 'the agreeable regularity of the plan' and his 'complete response to the demands of the programme', though admitting a fault in the 'comparative lateness of the style of the spires, and . . . of some of the details'. But Burges's internal decoration and fittings, his 'symbolic and hieratic art' demanded approval. His victory was a victory for 'Early Gothic', and what was more, 'Early French Gothic'. Scott pointed out 'it was the first occasion on which the Ecclesiological Society's law as regards Middle Pointed was set at nought'.

Competition entries, even unexecuted, might sway taste and make a name. After the Constantinople competition *The Ecclesiologist* announced 'Mr. Burges and Mr. Street have now proved their right to the highest rank in their profession; and Mr. Bodley and Mr. Slater (the Third and Extra prize-winners) have fairly won their spurs'. Yet, again, *The Ecclesiologist* showed a preference for Street's aisleless memorial chapel. Although they

'should have preferred a more gracious air and sentiment' they approved his 'artistic vigour' in an unmistakeably English memorial, which was itself 'the architectural monument, rather than the receptacle of individual memorials'.

Burges's view was that 'the church is essentially a memorial chapel, and should therefore be especially designed to contain monuments'. To that end he introduced a French type of apsidal chancel and ambulatory, while for the major part of his design he looked to the thirteenth-century S. Andrea at Vercelli, an Italian church which did however, according to legend, have a strong English connection. Burges's brilliant glazed tiles, mosaic, geometrical patterns in blue, black, red and white, and horizontal banding in red and white Mamora marble, would have responded gloriously to the intense southern sun. But it was certainly not English.

Clearly, competition instructions were important, but whether they should be more or less stringent, and allow for more or less originality was a contentious point. For Lille, the requirements were most specifically enumerated, causing the outright rejection of twenty-one entries which failed to meet them.

For Constantinople, the contestants were instructed to use a Gothic rather than Byzantine or Islamic style, to consider local climatic conditions, local availability of materials, and to avoid offending local sensibility in the use of figural design. A 'southern' pent-house roof shading the western portals was taken up by several architects; the reduction of window area, to some degree at least, and certainly the avoidance of large tracery windows, seemed an obvious expedient to provide a cool interior. Burges's first move was to 'ascertain what materials were to be readily found at Constantinople' as 'the design . . . must naturally be influenced by the properties of these materials'. He certainly intended to make the most of them. Others complained to *The Builder* that they had no source of such information, or that it was not clear to what extent Islamic culture should be deferred to. If the ringing of bells were offensive, should a bell-tower be included? Burges hoped to include an independent Italian type campanile, should future funding permit, which cleverly also recalled the lookout of the 'muezzin'. But all to no avail.

The requirements of international competitions encouraged study of continental Gothic. In 1844 Scott set out on his first 'continental tour' with 'unbounded' enthusiasm, specifically to study and sketch 'German Gothic' for his competition entry for the rebuilding of St. Nicholas's Church, Hamburg. He warned of the problems of travelling with 'lay companions' who had always 'done a place' when he had hardly begun. He was a conscientious student. Abandoning his friends 'I sketched pretty well everything at Altenburg to the very patterns of the glass', and 'I got a good day at Cologne, on which I half worked myself to death'. No wonder his companions had watched over him 'to see that I did not cause them to miss trains'. His efforts paid-off, the competition was won. By the mid-1850s Street was an assiduous traveller, turning his knowledge to good account. *Brick and Marble in the Middle Ages* was written after his travels in northern Italy in 1853, and revised in 1874. He praised the expanding railway system, but also suffered the tribulations of travel. Unable to find a bed for the night at Baden, he continued by road to Zurich, arriving 'just as day began to dawn' and a hotel was found. 'We were up again soon after eight . . . The main feature of interest for me was the Cathedral'. The student of medieval architecture needed not only enthusiasm, but energy.

In the second edition, Street explained his interest in North Italy in the early 1850s. 'We wished to combine the best architecture, the best painting, and the best sculpture in our works', and so looked south as well as north. Further, 'it was desirable . . . to meet the demand . . . for colour in construction' and Italy provided 'numerous ancient examples'.

Street was not the first to look south. Ruskin had followed *The Seven Lamps of Architecture*, 1849, with *The Stones of Venice*, 1851-53, and to Ruskin, Street acknowledged the debt of 'all who are interested in good architecture'. The demand for 'colour in construction' was taken-up in the 1850s at least partly in response to Ruskin's doctrines, although Ruskin himself disclaimed responsibility for the results. By admitting the use of polychrome, and the horizontal banding of William Butterfield (the so-called 'streaky-bacon' style), and Burges's glory of colour in his first design for Constantinople, Ruskin played a part in such liberalising of the Gothic Revival.

Restoration featured prominently in the Revival canon, engaging such notables as Scott, Burges and Slater. Early dogma led to many brutal 'improvements'. Scott recalled the Ecclesiologists had 'actually at one time doubted whether it would not be right to pull down Peterborough Cathedral, if only we could rebuild it equally well in the "Middle Pointed" style'. In fact, Scott's own, busy office, was involved in many 'improving' schemes. For Ruskin, 'that spirit which is given only by the hand and eye of the workman, can never be recalled'. His bias towards preservation was slow to spread, and the Society for the Preservation of Ancient Buildings was founded only in 1877, supported by new attitudes arising out of the Arts and Crafts Movement, and the activities of men like William Morris.

The subject of 'Town Churches' was reconsidered in the 1860s. A.J. Beresford-Hope, President of the Ecclesiological Society, argued for reconciliation of the needs of large congregations with liturgical function, within the Gothic form. Addressing the Annual Meeting of 1864, he recognized the limitations of the emphatic view that 'a church of the Church of England was to be a church and not a preaching-house'. He thought instead: 'it ought to be a church and a preaching-house too'. He cited Dutch examples, and advocated the adoption of large, unified spaces, of a wide nave, of narrow aisles, or no aisles at all. He questioned the need for a long narrow chancel, and even promoted the

introduction of galleries, the adaption of the triforium to accommodate the public. High vaulted structures would pronounce by their heavy mass their place in the urban environment. He met with some favourable response, but also some most hostile. Archdeacon Thorp was 'staggered' and 'upset'. 'It is all new, all heretical . . . exactly contrary to what we used to say.' Burges recognized the urban need, and suggested the 'Angevine churches, with great thick walls, domed or vaulted', as models.

J.L. Pearson had already embodied the idea of a massive, unified brick-built structure in St. Peter's, Vauxhall, due to be consecrated a few days after the Ecclesiologists' meeting, and also cited by Beresford-Hope. Despite Archdeacon Thorp's objections, the type was taken up and developed by James Brooks with a series of churches for London and its environs. Execution was still not guaranteed, of course. Christ Church, Clapton, designed in 1870, was another casualty of the architectural competition, but the heavy, spacious 'High Victorian' church had arrived.

The consideration of building and decorative materials had been significant since Pugin. A new respect for the traditional use of wood and stone was followed by the promotion of brick, after what Street called 'an ignorant prejudice' against it. Brick was to be used not just as a cheap expedient, but as a material with positive qualities. It was exploited in the constructional polychromy of the Butterfield type and lent itself well to the simple massiveness of the 'town church'. At Lille, Street himself had been praised by the judges for facing more 'boldly' than any other, the recommended use of brick as the main material for a cathedral.

There was another 'new' material to be considered – iron – 'new' at least in the extent of its availability. Pugin had approved the use of cast-iron where it acted as hidden 'ties' within a structure to give added stability. As Street said, every modern architect should exploit 'the intelligence of this mechanical age'. But while fine wrought-iron work was encouraged for furnishings, Pugin declared that the 'monotonous repetitions' of 'ready-made manufacture' such as cast-iron, should not replace craftsmanship. However in 1856, the Ecclesiologists promoted a design by William Slater for a complete 'iron church'. Iron was familiar as a material 'in railway-sheds' and buildings like 'the Crystal Palace', which 'fall within the province of engineering rather than architecture'. Now, the idea was to show how it could be utilised for 'a church-like building' without 'abandoning architectural forms (Gothic forms)' or 'violating' the properties of the material. Glaring faults of earlier efforts should be 'sent out to the colonies or erected as temporary churches at home'. Slater's design was intended as an adaptable 'blue-print', the ground-plan of which 'is capable of extension if necessary'. But there is no evidence of its having been taken up.

F.A. Skidmore, a building contractor from Coventry, passionately expounded the virtues of iron in a paper of 1856. He promoted cast-iron as a constructional material capable of realising the greatest height and span for a modern Gothic cathedral. He denied criticism that truth to the strength of the material necessarily resulted in unacceptably 'meagre' and 'thin' forms, and praised the crispness and delicacy of wrought and hammered iron for Gothic foliate decoration. His hope that 'some vigorous intellect' would erect an iron cathedral, exemplifying the 'metallic art of this *our* century' remained but a hope.

The needs of Empire extended beyond thoughts of mass-produced iron churches. New cities were developing and new cathedrals were required. Leading architects were called on, but again, there could be problems, and again poor Burges suffered.

In a scheme of 1859 for a cathedral in Brisbane, Burges combined a design based on 'Early French' with a character suitable to the 'semi-tropical climate' of Queensland. Boldly original, and with the Italian type tie-beams that were to feature in many of his later designs, it was, however, too costly for immediate execution. Burges hoped it could be built in instalments, and even 'in imitation of Notre Dame at Paris, that hereafter statues of our greatest kings and queens should decorate the west end in order to keep alive the connection of Queensland and England'. But in 1867, building was begun to other plans, those of D.W. Ryan.

Two competitions at home provoked great interest in the 1870s, those for the cathedrals of Edinburgh and Truro. In both, entry was limited by invitation, to three Scottish and three English competitors at Edinburgh, and to eight at Truro.

St. Mary's, Edinburgh, was to be in an 'essentially new part of the city' (Scott), approached through Melville Street. Yet again, the result proved very contentious. Scott won with a design of the early phase of the 'Early Pointed' style, which consciously referred to several Scottish 'noble examples', as at Jedburgh, Kelso and parts of Holyrood. Scott included a central tower and spire as an appropriately 'noble' feature for a cathedral, but one which was rejected by others as outside the reach of the £65,000

cost limit. Three other entrants were also clearly in the running, the familiar figures of Street and Burges, and one Scotsman, Alexander Ross. *The Building News* reported in January 1873 that Street complained that the winning design 'exceeded the allotted sum' while his own 'was within the mark'. The journal's own opinion of Scott's scheme was that 'it is scholarly, rhythmical, harmonious, but neither striking nor original'. The 'referee', Ewan Christian, appeared to favour Street, a view shared by *The Building News*, who praised his originality, but admitted 'the exterior lacks somewhat of beauty, as well as being intentionally severe, and is not equal in merit to the interior'. This was perhaps 'in consequence of over-anxiety to keep within the limit of the sum named'. Nevertheless, a vote for Street 'seemed more consistent with the views of the profession'. No wonder Street was somewhat irked by the result.

Burges came up with a much admired version of his favourite 'Early French', now refined from his experience of Cork Cathedral in Ireland. There he had won the competition of 1862-63, and actually saw his scheme built. One of the points against him at Edinburgh was practical. Ewan Christian pointed out that provision should be made for 1,500 people, and in Burges's scheme only 1,300 could be accommodated westward of the choir. While others might be placed 'in the choir aisles and elsewhere behind the preacher, it is hardly probable that all would hear satisfactorily'. The broad conception of Scott's plan allowed for 1,500 'westward of the preacher, and exclusive of the choir and its aisles'.

Ross's scheme was praised by *The Building News* as 'beautiful exotic', but 'not particularly suited to its purposes and position', and there were doubts whether it could be built for £65,000. It, too, was based on 'Early French Gothic', but the same journal went to some lengths to suggest that in his design Ross had 'consulted' Burges's ideas 'rather more without his leave than is desirable'.

In the event, Scott's eclectic scheme was built, an extra £10,000 being granted for the addition to it of two western towers, another reason for acrimony. The final cost was far in excess of that originally expected.

The difficulty of competition, for the architect, was highlighted by Scott who had, in fact, submitted at Edinburgh two full schemes, and a third, roughly drawn up. They were really variants of one idea, as he said, to provide the possible alternatives he would have suggested under non-competitive circumstances.

Awareness of the drawbacks of competition led to a peculiar circumstance at Truro. *The Building News* reported in March 1879 that all but one of the invited contestants expressed 'strong disapprobation' that 'a work of such dignity and importance should be degraded by being submitted to competition', and three, Burges, Pearson and Street, 'declined to submit designs at all'. After anxious reconsideration, the committee invited submission of drawings, not necessarily for Truro Cathedral. Drawings for earlier schemes could be entered, and would be judged as evidence of general ability.

PLATE
XII
PLATE
XIII
PLATE
XIV

St. Aubyn, Bodley and Garner, and Pullan were thanked by the committee for having prepared drawings expressly for Truro, and Brydon was assured the late entry of his design had not prejudiced his chances. Burges produced some fragmentary drawings, not submitted, which suggest he was thinking again of a thirteenth-century mode, very different from St. Aubyn's 'Early Geometrical of the fourteenth-century' or the ornate and unusual combination of features in Brydon's 'late fourteenth-century' scheme. *The Building News* admired Brydon's treatment of space on a rather cramped site 'when the congregational requirements of a modern cathedral are taken into account'.

It was, however, Pearson who, with no specific scheme for Truro, was judged the victor 'upon the merit of his completed works, or at any rate, the drawings for them'. The site proposed was that of the old Tudor church of St. Mary's, the south aisle of which Pearson was to incorporate into his plan. There was some regret at the demolition of the remainder of St. Mary's, but the appeal of the new Society for the Protection of Ancient Buildings went unheard.

Pearson, the victor at Truro, had a scheme of his own rejected, and rejected amidst uproar, elsewhere. Peterborough Cathedral was examined both by Scott and Pearson, and both were distressed by the crumbling state of its low central tower. In 1882 the tower noticeably moved: Pearson was summoned by telegraph. It was obvious that its piers were weakened, and the tower was dismantled, each stone numbered. In the course of this action Pearson noticed Norman work which indicated to him that the tower had been truncated in the later Middle Ages, and led him to the contentious proposal to rebuild the original Norman tower topped by a beautiful and archaeologically correct fourteenth-century spire. It was a gesture impossible to ignore but while the Dean was seduced, the Bishop and Chapter remained untouched by its appeal. Only when Archbishop Benson was involved did the Pearson spire founder, as he insisted on the rebuilding of the tower exactly as before. The conservative element was jubilant: 'we have escaped the misfortune of a nineteenth-century addition to Peterborough and that is the greatest gain' said the Society for the Protection of Ancient Buildings.

By the time of the Truro competition, and for the rest of the century, the freedom with which an architect might consider the Gothic style contrasted strongly with the strict attitude of the early 1840s. As Scott pointed out, that had served to focus 'the unity and consistency of the movement', but exploration of more diverse forms of Gothic, at home and abroad, had led to a succession of developments and moments of 'taste' in an architectural revival that seemed never to have stood still.

Pugin had said 'the beliefs and manners of all people are embodied in the edifices they raise'. He might have added 'and in those they design and do not raise', since some of the unexecuted schemes of the century could have proved amongst the most telling.

80 A. W. N. Pugin's Southwark Cathedral. Described by *The Builder* in 1848 as 'the most important structure which the English Roman Catholics have built in modern times', its final appearance was wholly unlike this initial design.

81 'Artistic Vigour' was the praise that *The Ecclesiologist* meted out to Street's competition design for the Crimea Memorial Church in Constantinople, though muted by the statement that it 'should have preferred a more gracious air and sentiment'.

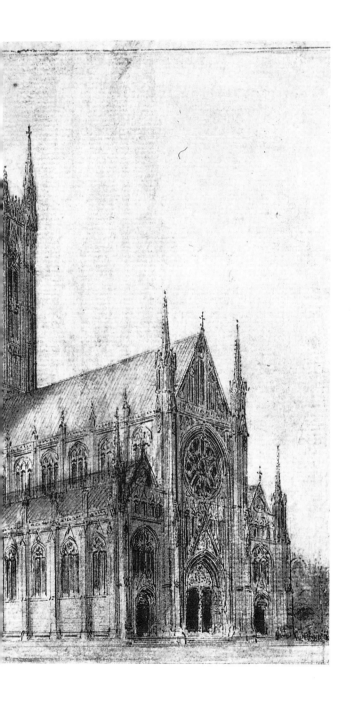

82 C. Brodrick's west elevation for Lille Cathedral. The architect most famous for the classical town hall at Leeds here produced a splendid essay in Gothic, which had typically French portals adorned with sculpture.

83 R. Pullan's entry for the Lille Cathedral competition. Its northern French style was obviously appropriate to the nature of the competition, but neither he nor Burges had the satisfaction of seeing his church built.

84 The interior of William Burges's entry for the competition for St. Mary's Cathedral, Edinburgh. The roofing is unusual in that typical Gothic stone vaulting was rejected in favour of beams.

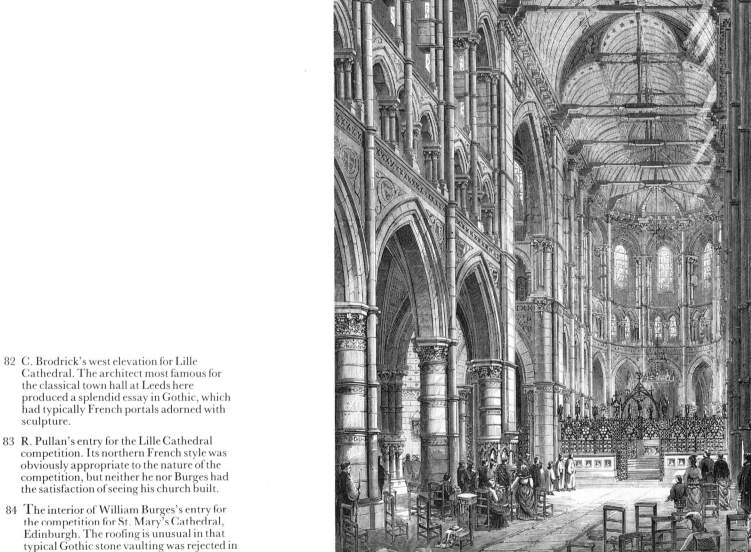

85 Medieval romanticism appears in Burges's submission for Truro, not only in the church itself but in the charming ancilliary buildings. To the right of the church is a tiny castellated structure that hints at his work at Cardiff.

86 Compared with the fine draughtsmanship on the central tower, the treatment of the rose window on the west front of Pullan's submission for Truro is slapdash. Attractive sculptural detail is suggested in the spandrels of the rose however.

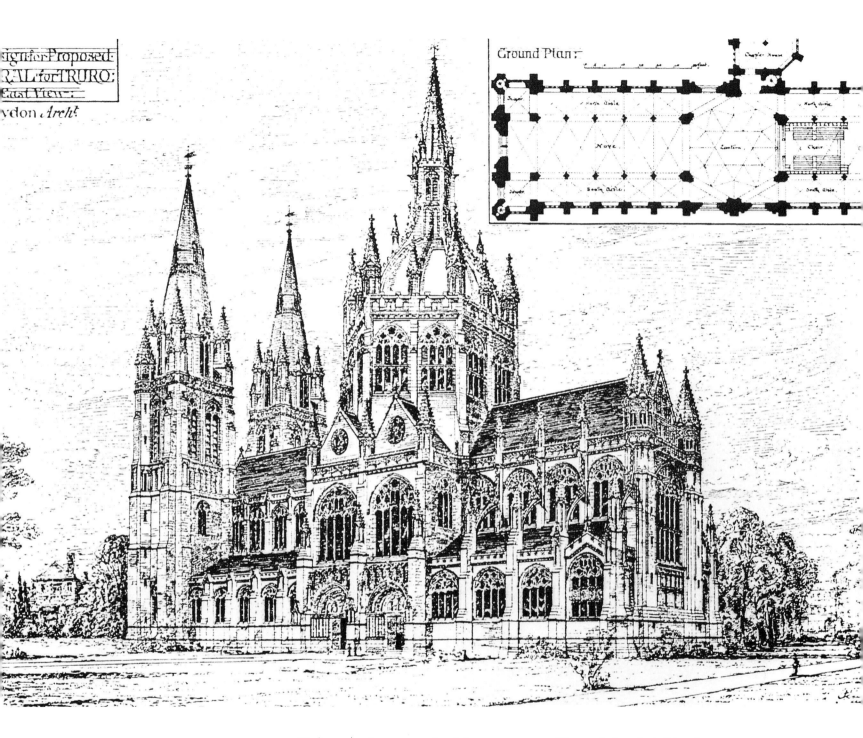

87 A crown spire, supported on flying buttresses is used in an extremely inventive way by J. M. Brydon for Truro. This spire, inspired by the fifteenth-century example at Newcastle, is typical of the adventurousness that Brydon applied to his design. Equally wayward is the use of double gables over the transepts.

88 The parish church which was destroyed to make way for Truro Cathedral. Its ornate Perpendicular carvings had been severely eroded by the time of the competition, but its destruction was controversial.

89 Pearson's winning design photographed c.1895. The whole surviving fragment of the parish church, St. Mary's Aisle, nestles against the bulk of the new building in the style of thirteenth-century Gothic.

91 Peterborough Cathedral from the east, photographed in the nineteenth century. When Pearson dismantled the tower he found fragments of Norman masonry which led him to propose a dramatic addition to the church. This prompted uproar.

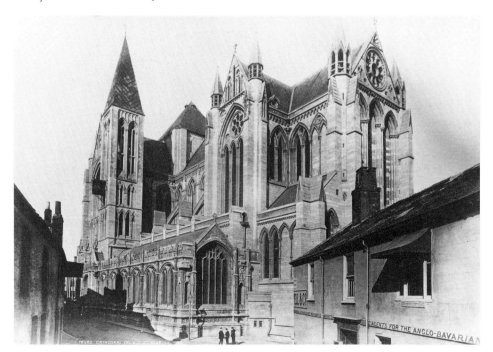

90 Truro Cathedral as completed, showing the Norman Gothic triumvirate of spires that Pearson used to give greater majesty to what was a small Cathedral.

92 Fierce argument surrounded Pearson's proposal to reconstruct the truncated Romanesque tower at Peterborough and to top it with a stone spire. When it was rejected, the conservationist groups that had opposed it were jubilant.

8. THE CATHEDRAL AGE IN AMERICA

'*T*he late nineteenth century was a golden age of cathedral construction . . . this "cathedral age" was in many ways a climax, some would say the last gasp of the Gothic revival.'

Thus the historian William Morgan pinpoints the worldwide enthusiasm for the building of Gothic churches on a massive scale. If the Old World offered the opportunity for restorations of and additions to ancient churches, the New World gave architects something more, the opportunity arose for cathedrals built entirely from new foundations. America was not dictated to by any existing cathedral nor, apart from a few dynamic, classical eighteenth-century churches, did it have a long-standing architectural tradition upon which to fall back. This gave freedom, but a freedom within the world-wide attitude to Gothic. A.W.N. Pugin's *Principles* had been published all over the world. None could doubt the importance of his argument that Gothic was the pre-eminent, the Christian, and therefore the *only* fit style for a church.

Or rather, more accurately, very few could. Pugin specified Gothic, others stretched the point to medieval, to include Romanesque. A defiant minority clung to classicism, and although they were never many, they were not entirely over-ruled. This would be true of cathedrals in America, as anywhere else.

One of the first great cathedral projects however, that for Albany Cathedral, fell thoroughly within the confines of the medieval. This project, for a vast cathedral in New York State, was conceived in 1873 when the New York State Legislature incorporated the Albany Cathedral of All Saints. That such a cathedral was planned was due, as in many other instances, to a dynamic and ambitious bishop. In this case, it was William Croswell Doane, appointed first bishop of Albany in 1868. On All Saints Day, 1881, he announced to his congregation that he intended construction of a cathedral as soon as possible. At this time the congregation had to meet in a building formally used as an iron foundry, which was entirely unsuited to its Christian purpose. The competition for Albany Cathedral was not open to hundreds of architects. Only two architects were involved: H.H. Richardson and R.W. Gibson. Richardson was contacted by the bishop in July of that year and was told to participate in the competition. Infuriatingly, the conditions and terms of the competition are now not known, but it seems from various communications that the Gothic style was actually specified. On a practical note it also seems to have been demanded that the building should be designed so that it could be built in two stages for financial reasons. The deadline seems to have been November 1882. Richardson went past this, submitting a design and an estimate for building the project in March 1883. Unfortunately for Richardson, it was felt that Gibson's design in English Gothic was more appropriate and this was accepted on 30th April 1883.

Why was Richardson's design rejected? Probably because it was going to be too expensive; however Geoffrey Carl Ochsner in *H.H. Richardson – Complete Architectural Works* puts forward the theory that the bishop had a predilection for English Gothic, whereas Richardson's design was for a massive cruciform church in opulent late Romanesque style.

The designs were published in *The American Architect and Building News* with a commentary:

> for this design, both in the interior and exterior, effect has been sought by simplicity of form and strength of mass, for which reason the main features have been kept very simple in outline, however rich the detail may be and the window reveals might have been made very deep. To obtain unity one consistent treatment has been used throughout the structure, while its different parts have such distinctive handling as they seem to demand. Certain strong features have been carried round the whole building, binding it together. The main entrances are by porches at the western end of the nave and at either end of the transept.

It was undoubtedly a design of great authority. The elevations of the west façade and of the south side of the church, published in *The American Architect and Building News* give us accurate impressions of what we have been denied. From the west there is a mounting composition: the large central tower with its polygonal low Romanesque spire and its well ordered Romanesque arcading is accurately echoed by the low western towers, each capped by short pyramidal spires. The Romanesque arcading on the western towers too is first class; slender, given several orders of moulding and entirely balanced. Lower down the façade there is more blank Romanesque arcading and the splendid heavy wheel window, precursor of the rose window, reminiscent of several in France in theory but in practice related to none. The entrances are reminiscent of Romanesque from Provence; St. Gilles du Gard immediately springs to mind when one contemplates the splendour of the three Romanesque doorways. The pyramidal spire motif and the polygonal roof are also echoed in smaller towers on the transepts and on small chapels flanking the west front. From the south, the longitudinal elevation of the church is equally happy.

With a sophisticated late Romanesque east end, with radiating chapels and ambulatory and transept façades related to those of the west end, Richardson had created a homogenous cathedral that was at once his own creation, yet entirely in sympathy with the late-Romanesque examples he had so carefully studied. He had travelled frequently in Europe and had been there when initially summoned to design the cathedral. But all this was to no avail. Richardson did not get to build the cathedral, that privilege went to Gibson.

Gibson's cathedral was very different, though it too had a low, central spire. It was in a much later form of Gothic architecture, dominated by windows. There is no denying that Gibson's church too is one worthy of execution, but Richardson's, whether it had been built at Albany or indeed anywhere, would have been one of the greatest churches ever built on the American continent.

Whilst Albany shows comparative orthodoxy of style, the designs for St. John in the Wilderness, Denver, conceived at the turn of the nineteenth century, are more engagingly divergent. Denver, Colorado, was an archetypal growth city of the period, expanding as America expanded westwards. The city had come to need a cathedral. The competition was won by the partnership of Tracy and Swartwout who submitted an interesting three towered design of late Perpendicular appearance. The competition entries for this virgin site varied not only in style but in quality. One of the less assured was submitted by the F.E. Edbrook Architectural Company. This was an elephantine church of indeterminate early Gothic provenance, but elements of a number of epochs were discernible in it, a squat pyramidal central spire with Rhenish overtones weighed heavily on a crossing tower with twelfth- and thirteenth-century elements. The transepts, pierced by simple rose windows, had a cresting of a vague geometrical shape. The west front however, supposedly the gateway to Heaven, had extraordinarily rounded projections where one would have expected west doorways and the actual doorways in flanking elements either side of the façade. This façade seemed to admit not to Heaven, but to a more mundane existence and the two towers above it were given a balustrade made up of crudely executed Christian symbolic motifs and are symptomatic of the confusion of the whole design. The perspective view gives the odd impression that the church was to be made of pressed metal sheets. It was a remarkably naive piece of design which seems ignorant of the refinements of architecture and the revival of earlier styles made in the nineteenth century, both in America and elsewhere.

More conscious of the analytical study of Gothic motifs in the period, is the design by Henry M. Congdon; an awareness of French and English Gothic is at once evident. This cathedral was to be entered through an imposing west portal, over which rose Christ in blessing, attended by angels, while other figures, possibly apostles or prophets, rose in series around the main arch. Above the gable of the doorway was a chaste set of five narrow lancet windows. Flanking the west front were two towers placed outside the aisles, giving a wide and proportionately low look to the church. And to give a deceptive impression that the building had evolved over a long period of time, the western towers were given different terminations. That on the south was flat-topped, that on the north given a crown of pinnacles to imply that it had a later completion date. Above these rose a central tower,

deliberately simple and grand in scale. There could be no doubt that this was meant to be a central tower of a major church. It was given a different balustrade again with stepped battlements, simple, plain but massive. It was an interesting piece of revivalism in that it showed a close knowledge of European antecedents, yet was immediately reminiscent of no known church. Nevertheless, for its period it was a little old-fashioned; it would have been unsurprising to find it designed in 1870, 1880 or even 1890 but by around 1900 other architectural forms had come to prominence.

This more contemporary approach to architecture can be seen in the suggestion of the architects Cram, Goodhue and Ferguson. Theirs too was a cruciform church but one with only one tower centrally placed. Their entire design was extremely unified, based approximately on the Perpendicular style but with great individuality. It was most reminiscent of the up-to-date Arts and Crafts style of architecture being practised in England and Scotland by architects such as G.F. Bodley. Indeed Bodley's masterpiece, the church at Hoar Cross in the Midlands, can be seen as quite closely related to this church. The American architects had chosen that medieval style where the vertical elements of the windows rose uninterruptedly to hit the main arch of the window and indeed on their west front two vertical lines, mullions, extended into small buttresses run through the window and beyond, continuing above the window to frame an architectural feature and a niche. The design of the windows round the body of the church, down the nave and across the transept all related very much to the design of the west window. But most fascinating of all was their use of broken pinnacles. Perpendicular was the period after all, where pinnacles bristled along the edges of major churches, on the chapel of King's College, Cambridge, or crowning the tower of Gloucester Cathedral. Here the elements which should continue into pinnacles, namely the buttresses between the windows, down the nave, and more noticeably the buttresses at the corners of the towers and on the intermediary flanks of the tower, do not do so. They are broken off as though the church has been left unfinished. This is a fascinating and an audacious thing to do to a church, yet something that is highly successful. There is no doubt that this is a very sophisticated piece of church design.

But perhaps there is one criticism. It is a sophisticated piece of church design but is it a sophisticated piece of cathedral design? Does it have quite the required degree of majesty? Bodley's church, at Hoar Cross, was after all, only a parish church and many of the greatest churches in this style in England were likewise. There was no great cathedral built in this style in England. Cram, Goodhue and Ferguson's church would have made an undeniably splendid adornment to a large and affluent turn-of-the-century suburb; but was it a cathedral?

There is no doubt that the design by another competitor was meant to be a cathedral. The partnership of Field and Medary produced a design that was as inventive as that of Cram, Goodhue and Ferguson, but a little more grand. Their church, cruciform like all the other entrants, did not have a central tower, but what it did have was a façade of great originality and ruthless plagiarism. Their church had a body that, like some other entries, was dominated by the Perpendicular style, but unlike Cram, Goodhue and Ferguson, they were eager to use pinnacles and little spires, vertical elements to give a variety to the outline. Down the side of the nave, and transepts were unusual flying buttresses, a feature unique to this design, not used at all in Perpendicular. Buttresses crowned not by early Gothic spires, as would have been the case had they taken their inspiration from Chartres, but by dumpy, Tudor domed pinnacles, repeated on a much larger scale on the transept façades. They echo those found, for example, around Henry VII's chapel in Westminster Abbey. But the most remarkable and free-thinking element of the design was the façade. Here two large towers rose up, dominated by vertical lines. Each of the two towers had four large buttresses which terminated in bristling pinnacles. These towers are exact replicas of the central tower of Canterbury Cathedral, the celebrated Bell Harry tower, which rose over the rambling mass of the great English cathedral. Here the architects have sensibly decided that if one of these towers is beautiful, two could be more beautiful; so the façade is made up of the central tower of Canterbury Cathedral repeated, as though in a mirror. Perhaps the weakness of their façade is the muddle below the level of the towers. There seems to be a large Perpendicular window, but it is flanked by two very bulky and inelegant buttresses. It is hard to believe that there was any structural purpose for these buttresses. Nevertheless it is a minor criticism of a design that shows originality and a real understanding of how to create a spectacular design on a comparatively small scale.

In total contrast is a competitive design by Frederick J. Sterner. This it would be kinder not to mention, as it seems to be a bizarre mixture of Baroque elements, mixed together in no known combination. Perhaps he can be excused by assuming that in taking elements of Spanish Baroque found in the Americas, he was trying to create a cathedral that had some American precedent, but the result is far from happy. Here we have a squat dome, rising in sections, on a polygonal base, echoed, it is to be supposed intentionally, by two very inelegant western towers. Less elegant still is the treatment of the façade between the two towers. The architect seems incapable of deciding what he wishes to do with this area and has simply flung in three windows, the central one given a rather odd tracery which seems to be a derivative of later Gothic. The whole church is, not at all successful, but it does show the diversity of styles felt suitable for a competition at the turn of the century: whether simple, primitive Gothic, whether equally primitive Baroque or much more sophisticated reinterpretations of Perpendicular in a wholly up-to-date way. Architects at Denver felt they had the option of designing however they chose. The Denver competition is important then because it shows that diversity was one of the most important features of a major competition in America at this time.

A cathedral which did not have a plethora of designs associated with it, but nevertheless could have been wholly different than it now it is, is Grace Cathedral in San Francisco. Early in the twentieth century the initial designs had been drawn by G.F. Bodley. A fascinating review of the church appeared in *The American Architect.*

> The cathedral planned to occupy the commanding site presented to the diocese after the great earthquake is . . . a Gothic building in the style of the fourteenth century. It was designed by the distinguished English architect, the late Dr. George F. Bodley, R.A., who completed the plans but a short time before his lamented death. Indeed, it is said he was occupied with them, almost to the very hour of his sudden passing away and that his last work was put upon them. His pupil and partner, Mr. Cecil Greenwood Hare, took up the work where he left off, in co-operation with the local architect Mr. George P. Hobart of San Francisco, who has large experience in building that city after the earthquake . . . The architect gives the dimensions of the church as 275 feet in external length . . . the width of the nave is 37 feet, the width across the nave and aisles, 120.4 feet . . . The central tower from the nave floor to the crossing of 144 feet high and to the top of the spire 270 feet from the ground line.

It was a cathedral which was thoroughly up-to-date in its construction: 'the architects explain that the construction of the roof might be of iron and that there might be iron rods or girders inside the beams so as to give extra strength'. The architect regarded it as 'very desirable that the cathedral should be built in stone ashlar of a good color, red or white.' The plans were referred to Mr. Hobart for further correspondence with Mr. Hare, 'touching such revision of the structural plans as might be needed to adapt them to steel frame construction'. And in explanation of this they referred to the peculiar earthquake conditions, citing a letter written to Dr. Bodley by the committee, in which it says: 'I think all experts here, as well as public sentiment, are of one mind that it will be necessary to make use of steel structure in view of our experience and the successful withstanding of earthquake shocks by larger buildings so constructed'.

In Dr. Bodley's reply he said, 'I quite fall in with the steel frame construction.' An unusual feature of Grace Cathedral's design was that there was no west door. Facing California Street was an imposing west façade, but the entrance to the church was via flights of stairs on the north and the south, leading to porches at the west end of the nave. Otherwise the church was fairly conventionally planned: cruciform with a central tower, transepts and square east end. The artist's impression, from 'the architect's drawing', published in *The American Architect* at this time, shows a church redolent of Wells Cathedral in the central tower and rather more original in the treatment of the west tower. Here are two slender structures, topped rather strangely by octagonal turrets and small spires. This is not the only design that the architects produced for the scheme. Perhaps the most imposing was one also produced by Bodley which showed a massive central structure, rather larger than a mere tower, which would have dominated the San Francisco skyline until the advent of the skyscraper. This large polygonal structure would have added enormous weight to the appearance of the church but also weight in the physical sense. Could it be that this would have been less suited to earthquake conditions? The cathedral progressed after Bodley's death under Hobart, and Hobart is responsible for the cathedral as it now is. There have been changes in its design; it is now more reminiscent of the west front of Amiens Cathedral with a large rose window and low western towers. The most serious omission is the lack of a central tower. Now we have a slender flèche, typically French but not as impressive and as dominating as the central towers that Bodley had originally proposed. But at least in Grace Cathedral we have a cathedral that was brought to a comparatively speedy conclusion. Here there were not the heart-rending competitions which invited designs by hundreds of architects, none of which were then built. At Grace Cathedral few architects were involved and although the design changed, one could call it an evolution rather than a rejection of better design. It is a comparatively happy note upon which to end. The

cathedral age in America gave us many types of projected cathedral: some, as Richardson's cathedral at Albany, lost masterpieces; others, such as the many rejected designs for St. John in the Wilderness, Denver, are more fascinating in themselves than they are worthy of erection. It is comforting to close with a building the design of which was conceived with comparatively little difficulty, and although changed over the years, has left San Francisco with an imposing and attractive cathedral.

93 Albany Cathedral as H. H. Richardson intended it to be, a brilliant composition in late French Romanesque. Horizontal and vertical emphases work together to create a grand and harmonious Cathedral.

94 The south elevation of Albany Cathedral, showing the relationship between the twin west towers and the massive central tower.

95 The ground plan of Richardson's church. The complexity of the ambulatory is evident, at the top of the drawing.

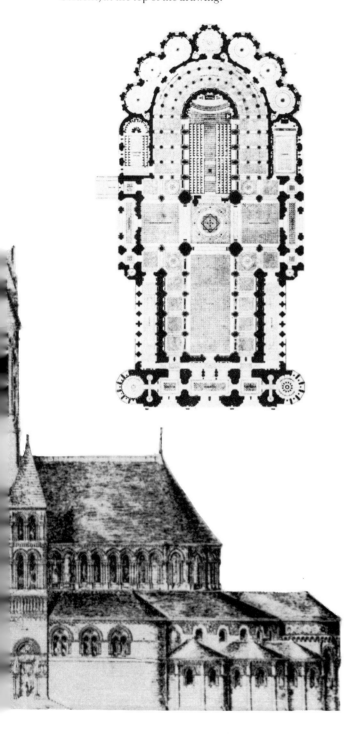

96 The winning design: Robert W. Gibson's Albany is a Gothic cathedral which lacks the majesty of Richardson's proposal.

97 The selected design for the Cathedral of St. John in the Wilderness, Denver, by Tracy and Swartwout, was an essay in the Perpendicular style.

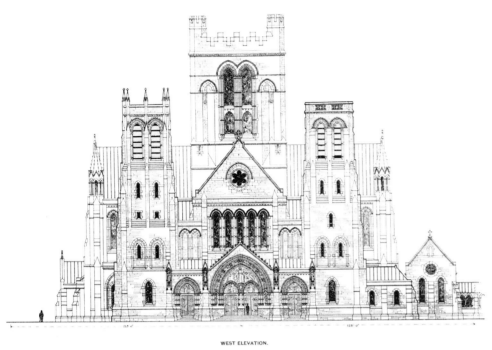

WEST ELEVATION.

100 Canterbury Cathedral improved. Field and Medary, appreciative of Canterbury's Bell Harry Tower, doubled it to make an audacious façade only slightly marred by projecting buttresses.

98 Henry Congdon's west front evinces a more sophisticated mind. The asymmetrical terminations to the west towers, designed to show the evolution of the building over a period of time, indicate an awareness of many medieval examples.

99 Arts and Crafts in Colorado. Cram, Goodhue and Ferguson submitted a reinterpretation of Perpendicular, which boldly eschews use of pinnacles. The resultant 'broken off' effect is dramatic.

101 The Bell Harry Tower, Canterbury Cathedral, the inspiration for Field and Medary.

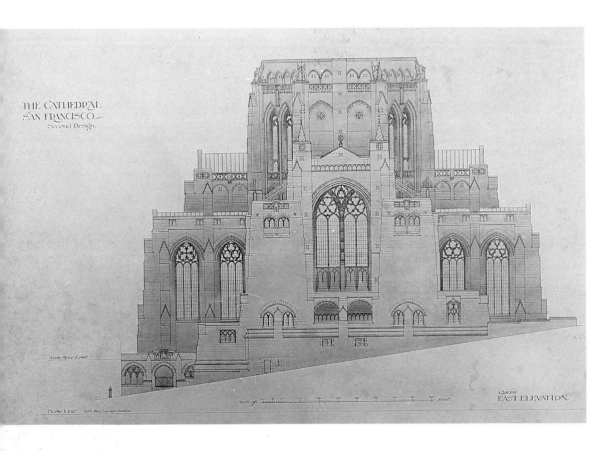

102 Grace Cathedral, San Francisco: west
elevation of G. F. Bodley's design which was
dominated by a large polygonal central
lantern.

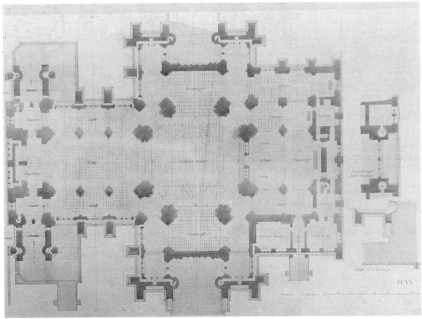

103 The ground plan of Bodley's church,
showing the intended central space.

I. Westminster Abbey with spires and cupola. This anonymous oil painting, of c.1734-40, has only recently come into the possession of the Westminster Abbey Muniments Room, and is based on several eighteenth-century schemes for completing the Abbey.

II. A view of St. Peter's, Rome, of c.1587, in fresco, by Pompeo Nogari. On the wall of the Vatican Library, it represents St. Peter's as imagined by Michelangelo, before the addition of the façade by Carlo Maderno.

III. Milan Cathedral appalled stylistic purists with the mixture of classical and Gothic in its façade, and in 1888 the generosity of a millionaire resulted in a competition. Daniel Brede submitted this Gothic version.

IV. A section of the dome showing the rich decoration characteristic of eighteenth-century France. Some of the details suggest that the design could be linked to the French Royal Family.

V. This watercolour of a French church remains, astonishingly, unidentified. Its unusual combination of section and west end views adds mystery to the controlled Baroque massing in the tradition of Mansard.

South Front Same Plan

VI. Sir Christopher Wren's Warrant Design for St. Paul's. When the innovative centrally-planned Great Model Design was rejected, the architect produced a longer church more reminiscent of medieval church planning.

VII. A design for a National Memorial Chapel by William Kent, now in the Victoria and Albert Museum, London.

VIII. Sir William Chambers's exquisite domed church which he proposed for St. Marylebone, London. Despite the finesse of his draughtsmanship, the project came to nothing, much to the displeasure of its designer.

IX. A detail of J. M. Gandy's drawing of 1825 which presented designs to the Commissioner for New Churches, showing the diversity of style considered.

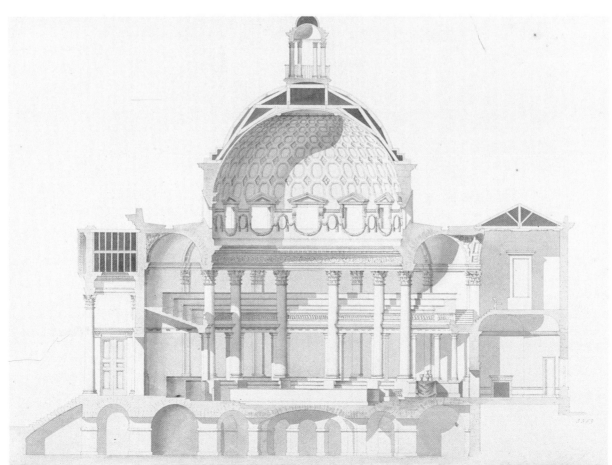

X. Almost nothing is known of the reasons behind this Gothic scheme by the Scottish architects Foreman and Cameron. With some echo of York Minster about its towers, it is most remarkable for the ogee dome that rises behind them.

XI. Nineteenth-century grandeur. The spire of this cathedral reminds one of Salisbury, while the evocative and persuasive watercolour treatment, now in the collection of the Royal Institute of British Architects, show architectural draughtsmanship at its most attractive.

XII. The Truro Cathedral Competition invited submissions both of new work and extant drawings. This highly-coloured interior by Burges shows a comparatively small church.

XIII. A Romanesque submission for Truro exhibits the opulence that was representative of Burges's style; now in the Victoria and Albert Museum.

XIV. More detail from Truro by Burges: wall treatment in a Gothic style shows a return to the use of paint that was considered typical of medieval design.

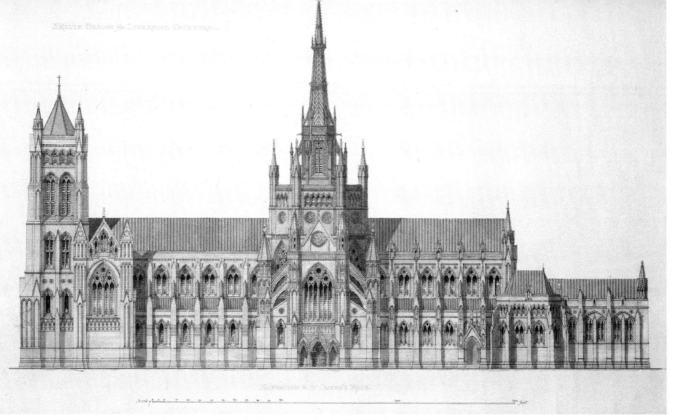

XV. Another member of the Scott family entered the competition for Liverpool cathedral in 1902. J. Oldrid Scott's entry was singled out for praise, but did not lead to his being among the five finalists.

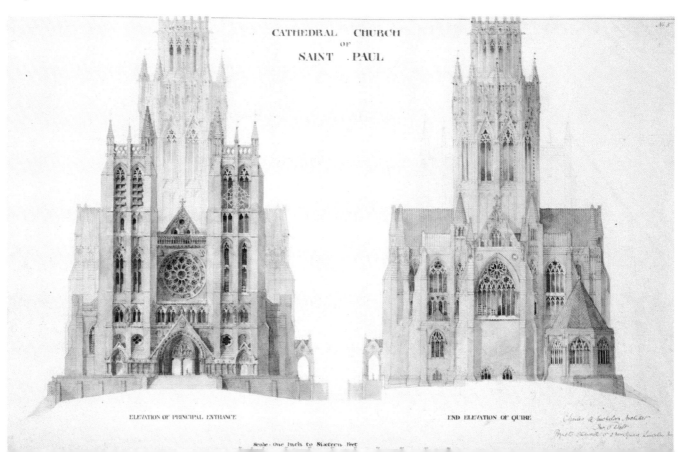

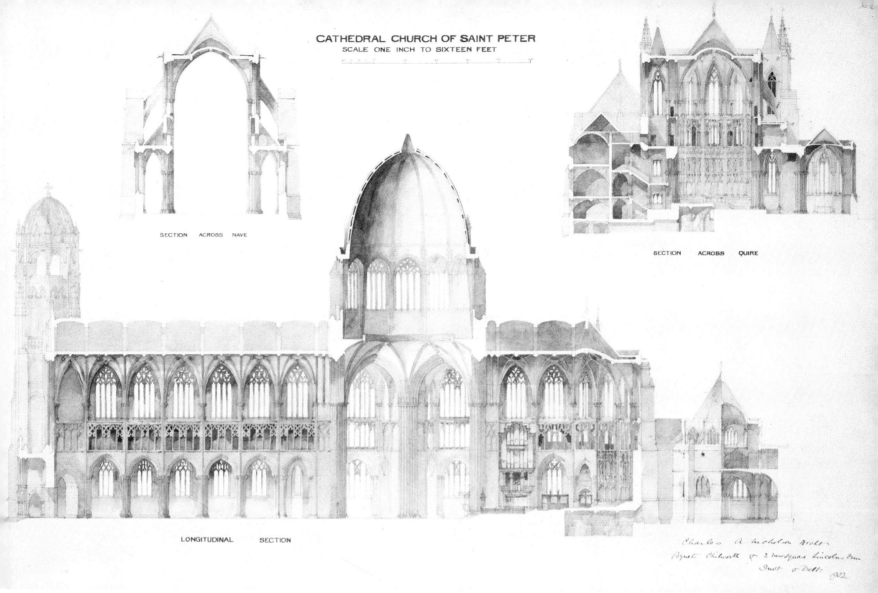

CATHEDRAL CHURCH OF SAINT PETER
SCALE ONE INCH TO SIXTEEN FEET

SECTION ACROSS NAVE

SECTION ACROSS QUIRE

LONGITUDINAL SECTION

XVI, XVII, XVIII. Three drawings by Charles Nicholson for the second Liverpool competition. His was a varied submission, with several different proposals. Perhaps the most extraordinary, and certainly the cause of much comment, was one characterised by a high central octagonal lantern, impressive inside and out.

VICARAGE GATE
KENSINGTON.
LONDON·W·
30TH·JUNE·1902·

Nº13A

XIX. Away from traditional material and design, W. R. Lethaby chose to use concrete for Liverpool, and suggested simple, vaguely Byzantine work, as shown by the blue interior of his apse decorated by angels.

XX. The model for Sir Edwin Lutyens's Roman Catholic cathedral for Liverpool. It shows the subtlety of his massing and was restored in the 1970s. It contributed greatly to the impact the Lutyens Exhibition of 1981 had on visitors.

9. 'SIMPLY ASTOUNDING' – THE CATHEDRAL OF ST. JOHN THE DIVINE, NEW YORK

The cathedral of St. John the Divine, New York, is still far from complete: a flight of steps leads to a portal that rivals the greatest of medieval cathedrals in its breadth and in the richness of its display. But above and behind this first layer of Gothic splendour there is much to be done. Building the church has been a persistently difficult process, and the choosing of an appropriate design proved as complicated and problematic; it has given us some of the greatest designs, and greatest lost opportunities, in the history of American architecture.

The project began easily enough. In 1873 Bishop Horatio Potter made the decision that the diocese of New York should have a cathedral, an understandable move in an age dominated by the building of massive new churches, both in America and Europe. In 1887 the site was acquired and soon afterwards the competition was announced. It was an open competition, without restriction, and the judges were soon faced with the creations of over sixty entrants. The styles presented ranged from a Mannerist domed cathedral by Edward Casey to a rather lumpen early High Gothic scheme by B.G. Goodhue; from a more attenuated piece of Hispanic Baroque by Carrère and Hastings, which had at least a vertical elegance about it, to a spindly Gothic one by Renwick, Aspinall and Russell, upon which rested a dome adorned with Gothic tracery in an almost Georgian manner. From these and from many others a short list of four was chosen: Potter and Robertson; Huss and Buck; Heins and La Farge, and the only individual in the four, William Halsey Wood. Their final drawings were handed in on 4th March 1891 amid rising public interest in the project, which was not without its scandalous side. 'Messrs. Potter and Robertson were at one time reported to have withdrawn from the competition quite at the last moment, owing to the comment which has, quite unnecessarily, as we think, been excited by the relationship of one member of the firm to the Bishop of New York' wrote the *American Architect and Building News*. 'As to the three other competitors' it went on, 'it is understood, we believe, that other persons, whose names do not appear, are associated with some or all of the competitors'. Of these it was the work of Halsey Wood which consistently attracted amazed attention. The journal informed its readership that there was every likelihood of the designs being put on display:

Meanwhile the public may content itself with the descriptions of the plans given by the reporters of the daily papers who have, apparently, not only seen them but studied them with an intensity and elevation of thought which put to shame the gross and material spirit in which architects contemplate such works . . . "Jerusalem the Golden" is the underlying motif of his (Mr Wood's) design . . . We should say that the timid members of the congregation would prefer to think that their church was based on a judicious application of the laws of gravitation and resistance which prevail in this sublunary sphere. But, as it also appears that "the Ten

Tribes, the Twelve Apostles, the Seven Churches, the Holy Gift of the Holy Ghost, the Four Evangelists, the Twofold Nature of Our Blessed Lord, Lawgiving and the Beatitudes" are among the analogies which have been entered into the plans we may hope that "Jerusalem the Golden" after all, is not to serve instead of a rock beneath the walls, but is only to appear as a subject of decoration somewhere upstairs. It would seem that the foregoing list might comprise motifs enough for one building, but we are informed that in the choir, the "symbolism of seven" is to prevail. As the choir is said to be seventy feet wide, and one hundred and thirty-five feet long, and contains one hundred and fifty stalls on each side, we suppose that the "symbolism of seven" is a little interrupted on occasions, but there are seven "chantries" attached to the choir, which shows that it is not entirely forgotten. The "chantries" which we take to be more properly chapels, as well as the nave chapels, have organs over the doorways, and we are assured that there is also to be a "great organ" which the reporter seems to confuse with a "choir organ" divided into two parts, which are to be placed respectively in the "north and west entrance towers". As the church runs north and south and is four hundred feet long the reporter appears to be quite right in thinking that "with supplementary orchestras effectively placed in the open spaces adjacent to the choir" and the "keyboard on the floor of the transept" the effect of the music will be "unprecedented".

Neither the anonymous writer nor the *American Architect* could resist similar attention to the creation of Heins and La Farge:

The same reporter seems to have devoted a part of his genius to the interpretation of their plans. In these, we are told in place, "the nave as a whole is to represent the Covenant". A little below, we learn that the "Church Militant" is "typified" in the nave, and, when we come to detail, we find that various portions of the nave are to be devoted to the Creation, the Last Judgement, the History of the World, the Messiah, and other various things so that we conclude that the architects have really only taken the sensible course of arranging the decoration of their building with some connected scheme, without losing themselves in the clouds of "symbolism" which float around newspaper reporters during their contemplation of plans of churches.

Sated by this jibe, the magazine continued in a more sensible way:

As to "symbolism" we will do all architects the justice to believe that, if such a thing occurred to them at all, it must have been an afterthought as no respectable building was ever yet erected without primary reference to the earthly materials of which it was to be built, whatever Father Durandus may have imagined. Speaking of earthly things, we are reminded to make the suggestion that even architects have an earthly as well as a heavenly part, and that, as there is very little probability that any considerable work will be done on the cathedral for a long time to come, it would greatly conduce to the maintenance in good order of the material portion of the competitor whose design is chosen, and indirectly, to the health of his spiritual part, if some arrangement should be made by which a reasonable salary could be paid to him during the long period of waiting for means to carry out his plan.

It was perhaps the *American Architect and Builder*'s own long period of waiting for the competition designs which exacerbated its critical mood. But the time of impatience was almost at an end. Two months later the journal published all four schemes not without further recourse to complaint, this time with due cause; for in its lamentations, it pointed out the slow and unsatisfactory workings of the judgement process:

> Instead of being one of the pleasantest professional events that has occurred in this generation this great competition has been one of the most disagreeable. A Board of Trustees was formed and they without the needed professional advice prepared the programme for the first competition, and when the drawings, made in supposed conformity with it, were submitted these Trustees endeavoured, for weeks, to make a choice. Finding that in some ways the task was beyond their capacity they *then* appointed a board of expert advisers, but later reverting to their first belief as to the superiority of their own judgement, they exhibited their appreciation of professional advice by including in the designs to which were finally awarded the first places, only one third of the designs recommended by the expert advisers adding to the list others which the experts had advised against. The loose manner in which the programme for the first competition was drawn by the trustees may be known from the fact that though it was supposed to call for "sketches" the experts found themselves unable under its terms, to throw out the fully rendered design submitted by Mr Gibson – which could hardly be thought of by anyone to be a "sketch"

One of the problems, that the *American Architect* is here so eloquently pointing out, is that of organising such a mammoth competition.

The competition for the Cathedral of St. John the Divine, New York, was not only celebrated for its final results, but for the disturbance it created within the architectural profession. And when the final competition stage was reached there was as much confusion as ever:

> One of the competitors submits to the unguided and unguarded Trustees a drawing at one tenth scale, in place of the one-sixteenth drawings understood by the other competitors to be called for and adhered to by them, and adds a highly coloured perspective to the black and white ones required, but finds an excuse for his action in the loose wordings of the programme. Another competitor has the fortune to be connected by ties of blood with the supposedly most influential Trustee who, to protect himself from any charge of nepotism has, according to newspaper reports, most unnecessarily done all in his power to prevent his relative from being allowed to enter the second competition, though he won the honor fairly as an unknown competitor in the first competition. A third firm are now being sued for $10,000 and have been

compelled to defend their right to use their design against an injunction suit, which vainly endeavoured to prevent the exhibition of its design, all because they declined to add to their own names the name of a third architect who claims an interest in the design. Against the fourth competitor nothing is lodged save the charge of plagiarism, which few can hope to escape. We do not think that this is pleasant record for such an undertaking and more than this, these facts have so impressed us, that we cannot feel there is any real meaning in the second competition. And hence that any discussion of the designs submitted in it will be barren of effect so far as the future building is concerned. It seems to us to be enough to lay before our readers the designs and the explanatory notes of the authors . . . for the designs submitted are, without exception, worthy of attentive study and consideration for all our purposeful conscientious and practicable solutions to the problem.

The magazine did occasionally have some good things to say on the Trustees' behalf. It pointed out to its presumably alarmed readership that the Trustees themselves were faced with mny problems not of their making. They were supplied with many technical reports on the project; 'much of this matter was quite immaterial to the main issue, some of it was the work of unbalanced hobby-riders and some of it was incubated by unquestionable cranks'. Nevertheless, it is likely that popular feeling lay not with the Trustees but with the architects whose designs had seemingly been so easily dismissed. When the plans and elevations were finally published for public inspection the interest they aroused must have been as much due to the circumstances of their creation, as to the elegance and subtlety of the designs themselves. Of a special interest both to those interested in architecture at the time and to later readers were the papers presented by the architects explaining their choices. All four competitors submitted not only their plans, as they had been requested to do so in the Trustees' instructions of September 1889, but a detailed statement in which all aspects of their designs were discussed. From these announcements the emphasis on the number seven that *The American Architect* had derided at a remove proved genuinely to have motivated Halsey Wood's choices, and a set of ground plans appeared in the press, annotated by the architect with the relevant lines from the biblical Book of Revelation which showed to all the depth and mystery of Wood's convictions. The other three competitors were less concerned with striking imagery than with supplying a reasoned account of the choice of style and disposition of architectural elements within the church and the materials to be used, though they too, felt that some reference to literature was called for. Potter and Robertson, inspired by Gerona Cathedral in Spain, cited the writings of George Edmund Street on the subject: 'The foremost English architect of his time and an unimpeachable authority, writes of this building in terms of the highest admiration.' Others favoured sacred rather than critical authors to bolster their cause – Huss and Buck's presentation opened:

> So build thy Temple that man
> In silent meditation of its grandeur
> Shall feel his soul raised to the
> Greater Glory of God

and concluded with the stirring

Unity! Mystery!
Majesty! Grace!
Stone upon stone,
And each stone in its place.

Heins and La Farge were content not to quote from others but to state in their own words the importance of iconography. 'Seated statues at the peaks of the great gables represent great teachers of mistaken religions, Buddah, Muhammed and Confucius being thus subordinated to the more perfect Christian faith.' Their entire church, as much as Halsey Wood's, was encrusted with sophisticated imagery and symbolism, not in a mystifying but in a logical and accessible way: 'the chancel is devoted to the expression of the fulfilment of prophesy in OUR BLESSED LORD and SAVIOUR. It should be the most impressive part of the sacred edifice and should be marked by its distinct architectural treatment: its proper adornment demands the highest effort of art, expressed in the most precious marbles, the most exquisite carvings and paintings and the finest mosaics and stained glass.' Their presentation both in word and on paper was convincing, and it was announced soon afterwards that their Byzantine design had won. Triumph for Heins and La Farge; disappointment for the others. For Halsey Wood disappointment is not strong enough a term; imbued with the conviction that his design was not only appropriate but right, he was devastated: 'I have been told that his failure to win the award broke his heart (I think this highly probable). In any case he died soon afterwards' wrote Ralph Adams Cram in 1936, about an architect whom he judged to be 'potentially one of the great architects of modern times'. In his view Halsey Wood's design was

 simply astounding . . . had it been built it would, I am persuaded have marked an era in the development of American architectural style . . . Visionary – impracticable and fantastic if you like, wholly original and combining instinct with tremendous vitality, it represented an emotional impulse that, I believe, could easily have been given a rational practicality if only the ecclesiastical authorities of the time had had the imagination and the courage to see their opportunity and to avail themselves of it.

But instead, they had availed themselves of the plans of Heins and La Farge and work began on their church. It was unquestionably a work of great splendour. Rising above the body of the church was an immense polygonal structure treated in the manner of a late Romanesque spire with attached buttresses and ·pinnacles. This dominant element of the church was echoed by two very fine spires in the same style at the west end while the circular movement of its walls was repeated in the large projecting apsidal terminations to both north and south transepts. It was, like many designs of its period, heavily evocative of certain medieval antecedents, but unlike many churches designed at the time had an ingenuity of planning and an appreciation of the majestic that made it extraordinary. Small towers, for example, flanked north and south transepts. In themselves these towers were large enough to adorn most medieval cathedrals, yet here they were used simply as tiny

elements of an overall design, made almost insignificant by the magnificent scale of the spire rising between them. The architects must have been thrilled when their monumental design seemed at last to be approaching realisation.

Work progressed, with an increasingly large number of problems, till the death of George L. Heins in 1907. The surviving partner, La Farge, had been the church's actual designer, but such had been the upheaval caused by structural defects, design changes and personality clashes that members of the Chapter were determined to use Heins's death to get themselves a more manageable architect with a more manageable plan. It was a terrible set back for a scheme that seemed, after many years of indecision and acrimony, on the verge of actually being built. But there was also the matter of taste: since the competition, fashion in major church design had veered away from Heins and La Farge's combination of Byzantine and Romanesque details towards the subtleties of later Gothic, a swing evinced by Vaughan and Bodley's anglicised designs for the National Cathedral in Washington D.C. Accordingly, La Farge found himself dismissed, replaced by the consulting engineer for St. Johns, none other than Ralph Adams Cram. Gossip had it that Henry Vaughan had been offered the position but had declined on the grounds that one cathedral was enough for one man, a rather grand piece of modesty. It is probably an apocryphal tale of the sort that so readily attaches itself to monumental and contentious projects. But nevertheless it would be very interesting to know how Vaughan would have handled the site.

St. John's under Cram and subsequent architects continued slowly and inexorably, the completion date always lost far in the future. Vaughan did design several chapels which have been built there, in his typical late Gothic style, and it is to be supposed that eventually a Gothic St. John's will dominate this corner of New York. While we wait, we can wonder what might have happened had Heins and La Farge's design been completed. Would it have proved completely impractical, given the number of structural problems that so quickly arose? And had they not won would Halsey Wood's marvellous monster be rearing its extraordinary head above us by now, or would another design finally have won out? The history of the competition for St. John the Divine is not only illuminating in its own right but, on a larger scale than most, typifies the problems experienced by both patron and architect when trying to organise a competition to produce a major cathedral at the end of the nineteenth century. At St. John's, we are singularly fortunate in possessing details of the architects' response to the problems and the demands of the brief. All the architects seem to have understood that a Protestant cathedral for a Protestant form of worship needed a large central space for preaching. At the same time they favoured a style of architecture which had not previously produced such a manipulation of space. In their combination of old architectural styles with a new form of church, the designs for St. John the Divine show us not only dexterity in the handling of ornament but dexterity of planning. Contemplation of these four designs rarely fails to produce speculation on the part of the onlooker and it is speculation fired by some of the most intriguing plans ever proposed for a church.

Competition Design for the CATHEDRAL of
St. John the Divine New York
Carrère & Hastings architects

105 Robert W. Gibson was the winner of the
Albany Cathedral competition, but his
mammoth Gothic pile for St. John the
Divine was less successful. With towers at
both west and east ends and an openwork
central spire, it was a Gothic fantasy on the
largest of scales.

104 The submission by Carrère and Hastings
exhibited a dizzying verticality and a pair of
towers quite unlike any previous church.

106 W. A. Potter and R. H. Robertson's
perspective for the competition.

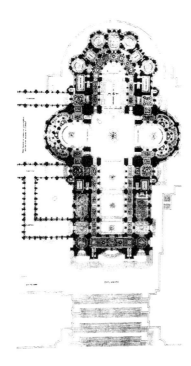

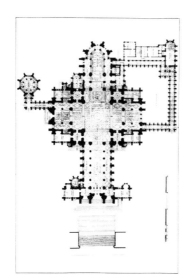

107 Ground plan of Potter and Robertson's design.

108 The winner. Heins and La Farge's church lacked the audacity of Halsey Wood's design, but seemed more likely to be executed. Nonetheless, it too was swiftly abandoned.

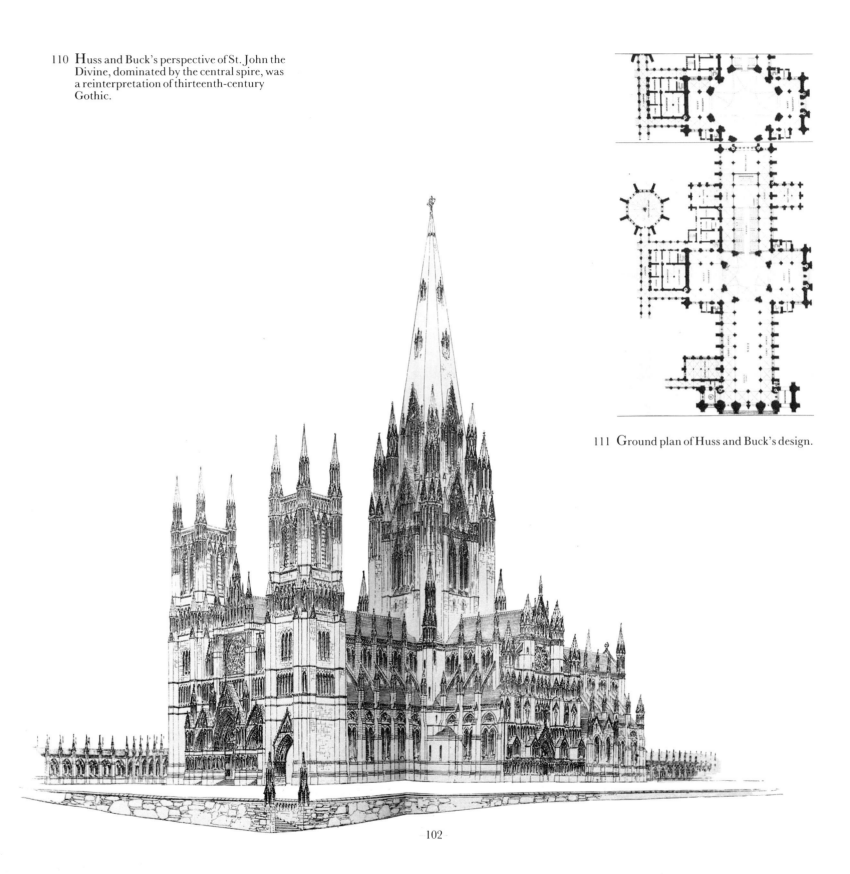

110 Huss and Buck's perspective of St. John the Divine, dominated by the central spire, was a reinterpretation of thirteenth-century Gothic.

111 Ground plan of Huss and Buck's design.

Competitive Design for the Cathedral of
St. John the Divine, New York
W. Halsey Wood, Archt., January 1890

113 Halsey Wood's ground plan.

112 Halsey Wood's design. By far the most inventive or insane submission, depending on one's point of view, it exhibits a medieval vision that would have been amongst New York's grandest buildings.

10. LIVERPOOL CATHEDRAL — 'A WHOLESOME WARNING TO ARCHITECTS'

*W*hen the diocese of Chester was founded in 1541, it covered a large area of the North West of England noted mainly for its rural emptiness and its recusancy. Of its many small towns, Liverpool was one of the least populous. By the late nineteenth century the situation had completely changed. Liverpool had a population many times that of Chester; it was amongst the world's most affluent ports and centres of commerce, and for both reasons of practicality and pride, required a cathedral.

Liverpool became a separate diocese in 1880, when the very unimposing parish church of St. Peter was elevated to the rank of cathedral, a role to which it was entirely unsuited. The precedent of pious splendour set by our medieval churches very naturally inspired a desire amongst the Liverpudlians for a building conceived from the first as the seat of a major bishop, to replace one surprised by its sudden dignity. Soon, in 1885, an Act of Parliament was passed which incorporated the Liverpool Cathedral Committee and authorised the building of a cathedral on a site, then occupied by St. John's church, immediately to the west of St. George's Hall. It was a site where urban magnificence was already well established: St. George's Hall, the libraries and art galleries, the public display of the city's wealth and culture, described by Sir Nikolaus Pevsner as 'The finest neo-Grecian building in England and one of the finest in the world' – were, and still are, an assembly of immense classical public buildings which must fleetingly have given the visitor, newly emerged from Lime Street Station, a passable impression of being in the Roman Forum miraculously restored. Those concerned with the project (and they were many, as a competition was announced for the design), agreed that St. John's would not be missed: 'A church of little architectural interest', said *The Builder*, curtly. They were also unanimous about the importance of the chosen area. *The Builder* indeed, to give its reader an immediate impression of the possibilities, produced a vision by H.W. Brewer, which showed, rather improbably, Notre Dame in Paris, its defects ironed out, framed by the curving colonnades of its neighbours. Brewer's view was of a slightly different site, one which allowed both St. George's Hall and the cathedral some *lebensraum* in which to breathe. St. John's, closer to the vast classical hall, was cramped by comparison, and the idea of jostling against St. George's Hall was not a happy one. More useful was the challenge this site offered: being wider than it was long, it suggested a departure from the usual nineteenth-century practice of a long nave. But as the press said, 'modern church worship, unless from the point of view of a small section of Churchmen who are as archaeological in their religion as in everything else, is essentially different from medieval church worship'. The slope of the site was a cause for potential excitement: 'it creates difficulties in some respects, but it almost compels a bold and effective treatment of the western façade'. In deference to St. George's Hall, *The Builder* opined that a scheme based on Wren's Greek Cross design and Great Models would suit, but as it said, 'Dis aliter visum; the selected competitors think otherwise.'

There were three competitors: James Brooks, the partnership of Bodley and Garner, and G.W. Emerson, all of whose designs went on display in Liverpool, together with a design by James Hay, a 'clever and energetic local architect'. The interest they caused was intense; visitors of all classes filled the hall, causing queues before the most beguiling views. One Saturday evening the gallery opened till late to accommodate the working classes, and 800 workmen visited it to view the designs.

As for the designs themselves, their instigators had specific reasons for their choices of style, all of which were published: Brooks began his proposal with propriety, suggesting a monument on the doorways of the south transept, bearing the names of those whose remains had been interred in St. John's churchyard. As regards the living, he was concerned to accommodate the largest possible congregation without detriment to the view of the preacher and chose a wide design, lit by a central lantern. This need for space for huge crowds influenced his planning in the upper parts of the building, where a large triforium gallery above the main arcade was available, as 'particular occasions may arise, festivals, for instance, in a large city like Liverpool: when this extra accommodation may be very desirable'. His style was unequivocally Gothic, and was admired as such by critics. His plan was medieval, made more practical for modern needs, a permutation which prompted some musings on planning: to make a medieval plan entirely practical for modern worship was impossible.

 But practicality is not everything in a cathedral. Architectural effect and impressiveness are a very important part of the objects of such a building, and a cathedral which seated all the worshippers in the most commodious manner for hearing and seeing, and left them totally unimpressed by any dignity or effect in the architecture, would have fulfilled only half its purpose. Association, again, is strong in these matters; stronger perhaps than in anything else. We are, as Tennyson perhaps rather bluntly puts it, "the fools of habit" in religious ordinances and surroundings, and the form of building which was impressed on one as a church exercises a certain glamour over us; we cannot feel so fully "at church" in a building of another shape and of other associations.

Whether the Liverpool cathedral should be a medieval building or not depends on such a variety of considerations and influences that it is difficult to form any opinion one way or the other.

But it may be reasonably urged that a cathedral should promote the greatest happiness of the greatest number of those who are to use it. Whether a modern Gothic cathedral is the form most likely to effect this end, we should feel it very rash to predict. We confess to a doubt on the subject. But if it is to be supposed that it will do so, there is no doubt that the design before us has very high claims.

Bodley and Garner also submitted a Gothic plan as they were very much aware of the responsibility that rested on the architects called to design the greatest new church since St.

Paul's: 'We think that no trouble or expense ought to be spared in order to make this present work as great a success as Sir Christopher Wren's noble church is admitted to be.' With this sense of history guiding them, they could not but choose 'the national style, in which our cathedrals, except this one (i.e. St. Paul's) are erected, and which is so intimately connected with an Englishman's idea of a cathedal. 'Sir Christopher Wren', they confidently continued, 'shows great leanings towards these ideas and we have no doubt that, had he lived in these days, he would have designed such a work in the English rather than in the Italian manner.' Having vouchsafed St. Paul's almost by default, they looked to it with admiration for its Protestant plan, affording the central space that was so necessary to current religious practice. Rather annoyingly medieval, or to use their phrase, 'national' styles were at first incapable of furnishing a similar example, till they hit upon the one exception:

> Fortunately one of our old English cathedrals shows how this useful feature can be adopted in the national style, and in the octagon at Ely we have the same arrangement, treated most successfully in the English manner, by the celebrated Alan of Walsingham.

They then stated their case: Ely's octagon was a mere adaptation of an older church. Their proposal offered:

> the advantage of an entirely new design, and we think that the octagon that we propose, with its eight nearly equal arches, would produce an interior effect which has not been obtained, as far as we know, in any cathedral yet erected in the world. The style we have chosen is that of the early fourteenth century, and is of strictly English character. We cannot but think that the beautiful manner of our Engish architecture should be displayed for this which will be the most important ecclesiastical building that has been planned for many generations in England.

And their self-assertion was as evident in the scale of the church as in its form: Liverpool, being so populous and important, deserved the best, the best in this case being a cathedral 110 feet high inside, taller than any medieval English cathedral. Of the aptness of their type of Gothic, Bodley and Garner were in no doubt. Theirs was an ornate type of architecture, and they were at pains to choose a hard resilient stone for the exterior in order to meet the competition's requirement that the proposed cathedral should stand up well to the 'smoke and chemical action' of the industrial north.

It was a design well proposed, and one well received to a point. Bodley and Garner's appreciation of the medieval was beyond dispute; the influence of Ely, and of Lincoln, was evident. But the strict adherence to the strong narrow medieval plan was not the cause for unanimous praise: it was thought to be *too* medieval. In the view of *The Builder*:

> It seems to us a matter for regret that a modern cathedral should be built merely as an imitation of an ancient one, and with no attempt to work out new ideas and materials in a new form. But we say this in full recognition of the admirable way in which the authors of this design have treated it from their own point of view.

On the other hand, their sensitivity to the cathedral's surroundings (those beautiful albeit 'Italian' buildings) was more easy to accept. It was, finally, a graceful rather than a powerful church that they advocated, and power and strength were perhaps the more desirable characteristics.

Strength was very much an element of the robust design by the third competitor, Emerson. Robust could equally well describe his presentation, which examined the concept of cathedral design, use and style from every possible viewpoint. His submission was accompanied by scores of photographs of extant cathedrals – Florence, Rouen, London, Rome and many more, as tools in his persuasive arguments concerning the relationship a modern cathedral should have with its site and its neighbours, and more generally how it should contribute to the skyline, how it could perform as 'a portion of the *coup d'oeil* of the city in which it is erected'.

From his lengthy and exhaustive researches, Emerson concluded that the long medieval type of church (as selected by Bodley and Garner) was incapable of supplying the desired grandeur on the site available to Liverpool. This he illustrated with photographs of distant views of London and Paris.

> Westminster and Notre Dame stand out with no especial prominence, while St. Paul's and the Pantheon impress the eye at once. In Edinburgh the new cathedral, even where one can command a full view of it looks unimportant, not to say unimposing, and from the city it is scarcely seen at all . . .

> To secure the effect of mass, a treatment differing from the long and narrow Medieval one is necessary, and imperatively called for in the case of the Liverpool Cathedral. I consider the pyramidal form of grouping, with the grand domical central feature, to be the best:–
> 1st. Because its mass, in combination with its height, gives the greatest attainable grandeur and impressiveness.
> 2nd. Because it best ensures the execution of plan essentially adapted to the modern requirements of the cathedral service.

> Liverpool itself, indeed, may be said to have no distinctive cathedral associations; but the people are English, and have memories which connect themselvs with the beautiful medieval churches of the country. Accordingly, while, to suit the city and the requirements of our modern service, a new departure is desirable, and should be made, the architecture, out of respect to the sentiment of the people, should follow the principles and express the feeling of our grand old Gothic cathedrals. To effect this combination, and design a cathedral which shall be worthy of the second city in the British Empire, has been my aim in the plan I have submitted.

This led to the vital choice of architectural style. Like his rivals, Emerson was at once aware of the presence of the gargantuan St. George's Hall. Medieval planning was no longer appropriate, he felt, but its architectural style most definitely was:

> Some might think that the surroundings demand a Classical or Renaissance treament. To my mind a style

of building based on this idea would be a great mistake artistically. The scale of St. George's Hall is enormous; and a cathedral of similar architecture, holding its own in respect of detail, would require to rival St. Peter's at Rome in magnitude; and this would only overwhelm the Hall, a building which the cathedral should enhance and not extinguish. A further cogent reason why a Classical architecture should not be adopted is, that it is pagan and un-English in origin, while Gothic is Christian, and, more, our national style of architecture; and, whatever may be done in the matter of our civil or municipal buildings, surely our religious edifices ought to serve the Christian character that they have had for ages. The style to be adopted should have harmonious contrast with the surroundings, edifying, not annihilating. It should be very simple and dignified. Such a style is to be found in a very early phase of the Gothic, when it had shaken itself free from the trammels of Classicism.

His choice was a noticeable contrast to the spiky later Gothic spires and pinnacles of Bodley and Garner. His simpler forms echoed, as he said, Loches, Périgueux, Angoulême, churches rather more Romanesque than Gothic. Romanesque, in the literal sense, was the interpretation that he wished to put on Gothic: these churches were 'the nearest approach to the classic feeling found in Gothic work, which is exceedingly beautiful'.

More than the other architects, he examined the demands of ritual on the plan:

As the mystery affected by the religious bodies in the Middle Ages, and which enforced their separation from the congregation and partial concealment by choir-screens, &c., no longer exists, and modern feeling demands that the largest number shall be admitted to see and hear the services that are specially intended for their benefit, without being impeded by large piers, it is necessary that the construction be such as to ensure an excessive unbroken area in the interior.

I have, therefore, added to the nave and transepts, of the great width of 53 feet from centre to centre of the arcade walls, an open space in front of the choir and pulpit of about 9000 superficial feet, exclusive of the accommodation in three galleries, containing 1200 superficial feet.

By the plan submitted, nearly 1400 persons can be accommodated in the unbroken area within 100 feet of the pulpit, exclusive of the gallery accommodation.

A Gothic vault over such an area of, say, about 100 feet diameter, and of proportionate height, would require abutments out of all proportion, and be excessively expensive. A Gothic dome, on the other hand, properly constructed, is self-supporting, and has no thrust, and but little tensile strain. It can, moreover, – an important point in regard to economy, – be erected without centering, which a vault cannot.

And of course a dome satisfied the Emerson craving for splendour. In case there might be those who would question caustically the veracity of a Gothic dome, Emerson rather desperately cited the 'beautiful Mohammedan domes so common in the East' which 'are practically Gothic'. Away from constraints of epoch, his claims for the majesty of the idea were on surer foundations:

A dome is impressive internally in proportion to the inability of the eye to measure it, as, in the Pantheon, in St. Peter's, in Sta. Maria del Fiori, in Sta. Sophia, and in the Gol Gomuz. This property gives it vastness; and grandeur is unattainable without a sense of vastness.

On his chosen ground, he felt capable of criticising any previous church which fell short of his standards. While others bowed deferentially to St. Paul's, Emerson faced it unconstrained by reverence. Its admitted beauty was marred by the narrowness of the nave in proportion to the dome, and the upsetting and inelegant springing of the circular arches under the pendentives. These faults could not be helped: they were Italian not Gothic. Had Wren designed a Gothic dome, he would have found a lovelier solution. Since he had not, Emerson now supplied it. His presentation, continually broken up under numbered headings, had the relentless conviction of one who knows that he is right, always supported, as if it were necessary, by relevant fact. Narrow naves were unsuited to modern sermon. To dispel any doubt, he put forward the sad instance of the mourning service to General Gordon in Westminster Abbey. For fairness's sake, he recruited a third party, the *Pall Mall*, which reported that 'The Dean gave a suitable address, but the greater number of those present could not join in the services.' His western towers were placed outside the aisles, with a porch or narthex between them. His reasoning was methodical and brooked no argument.

The reason of placing the towers outside instead of at the ends of the aisles is threefold:–
1st. To avoid the painfully contracted effect produced by two tall towers immediately flanking the nave, as in the case of the cathedrals at Cologne, Chartres, Rouen, Brussels, Lichfield, York, the abbey at Westminster, and a number of others.
2nd. To obtain a grand spreading west elevation with the dome well visible in the rear.
3rd. Because in the view from either side of St. George's Hall, the whole length of the nave is seen, whereas one bay would be hidden by the towers if they immediately adjoined the nave. The greatest effect of length is thus obtained. The cathedral of Cologne is a notorious example of how a long church can be spoiled both on the west façade and side views by the towers immediately flanking the nave.

Equally assured when discussing construction and even acoustics, Emerson's long submission was by far the most self-confident. Excerpts posted in *The Builder* proved his determination to clarify every possible question which might be raised. And it was unarguably original, perhaps *too* original!

The design as a whole is unquestionably a remarkably bold and original one; it has merit, so unhappily rare in modern architecture, of being a departure from mere precedent, an effort to think out a design in a form suitable to the special circumstances of the case.

This departure from ecclesiological precedent has

already, we observe, been made the subject of local attacks emanating from the Medieval church party, who apparently think it the greatest merit of a modern cathedral that it should resemble an ancient one. The reasonableness of this view, as we have before suggested, depends on whether the cathedral is to be regarded as built for a church which is to remain established on Medieval lines of thought and sentiment, and ritual, or whether it is to be regarded as the abode of a modified modern worship, suited to the spirit of the present day.

All we wish to point out is that objections to this design for not being on the orthodox Medieval pattern only hold good on the theory that the church is to remain on the orthodox Medieval pattern. In regard to the purely architectural view of the matter, the design appears to us to be a striking, grand, and original one in its main idea and composition.

However, *The Builder* was not entirely won over, raising the valid point that the exterior, despite Emerson's earnest protestations, gave an *impression* of classical rather than Gothic architecture, while the Gothic details themselves were too heavy. Fears were subtly expressed about the towers' Mohammedan antecedents: while the author claimed a precedent at Peterborough Cathedral, to the reviewer they were 'minaret-looking'. In its most astute observation the journal opined:

> We cannot help feeling that the architect might have done more justice to his very bold conception if he had treated what is in reality a Classic composition with a more Classic form of detail; in fact, that means to be a Classic design, but somehow or other has worked itself out Gothic.

Emerson's submission was thus accurately assessed by *The Builder*. Tenuous indeed was his attachment to the form of Gothic design. Yet Gothic was the only factor to unite the competitors; they had submitted three different designs and three very different arguments. Variety and excitement won out: first prize was awarded to Emerson. All seemed set for a domed cathedral in Liverpool but, within a few years, problems had arisen. By 1888 the proposal was abandoned, leaving Liverpool without a cathedral, and architects without any faith in the value of competitions.

A decent interval elapsed; to revive the idea of a Liverpool cathedral needed skill and determination. Both were found in Dr. Chavasse, the bishop to succeed Bishop Ryle in 1900. By October of that year he had already formed a committee to investigate the issue of site, since that had so noticeably undermined the previous competition. Of four potential locations, two were soon discarded, two others – the Monument site and St. James's Mount – were more likely. Both had passionate supporters and opponents. The Monument site, nearer the centre of town, had more support but was finally rejected because of the cost involved. St. James's Mount, away from the commercial heart of the city, was more affordable and was the eventual choice.

The controversy surrounding the site naturally spilled over into the competition. In Autumn 1901, architects were invited to submit portfolios of their work, not necessarily designed for Liverpool. The committee in charge stipulated that Gothic be the style, which at once raised the hackles and voices of those with an opinion on architecture. The press derided it as a 'foolish and mischevious resolution'. 1902 was too late to impel adherence to Gothic Revivalism.

> Here is the ecclesiological prejudice in church architecture in full blow again; a great chance for the production of a grand and original piece of modern church architecture is deliberately thrown away, and we shall have another specimen of imitation mediaevalism. Not only is the Gothic style unsuitable for a modern cathedral; the fatuity resides in demanding a special "style" at all. Architects should be invited to design a cathedral, simply, and be left to consult their own genius as to its treatment. A Committee who could make a formal demand for a "Gothic" cathedral must be entirely behind the age in their ideas, and entirely ignorant of the spirit and tendency of the best modern thought in architecture. By making such a demand they have practically thrown away a great opportunity . . .

A leader article in *The Builder* entitled *The Ideal of the Modern Cathedral* stated the current view:

> Nearly all our mediaeval cathedrals were originally built as a portion only of a great clerical institution which, though, it has its survivals, no longer exists as a part of our national life or of our national Church. They were built for a worship carried on by the clerics of the choir, and not partaken in by the laity. The long nave was nearly useless except for occasional processions, but its grandeur, and that of the west front, were regarded in the light of an offering, an architectural praise of God; Now a modern cathedral is nothing of all this. It is not connected with a great religious establishment requiring a train of buildings grouped with it. It is not erected for an exclusive worship carried on by the clerical body on their own behalf. It is mainly a great church, principally built for the worship of the laity, with a service conducted by a limited number of priests. You may choose to build a cloister for the sake of effect – but its practical necessity or utility has gone. The modern cathedral, then, is simply a great church, the mother church of the diocese, with a special official significance in that sense, but otherwise a church for public worship in the same sense as the parish churches. But there are two different theories on which the plan may be treated. We may regard the main space of the plan as the church for worship, in which case there must be the possibility of hearing or we may regard the main space as a place of meditation only, and a place of monuments to the righteous who have departed, and as the vestibule to the actual place of service, which would be restricted to more manageable dimensions. This is actually the case with the mediaeval plan; but the mediaeval plan, with its character of length without breadth, and its restricted

spaces in the choir, is most emphatically not the plan for a worship which has become essentially congregational, not merely priestly. There is nothing so grand in effect, if we want this idea of floor space, as a circular form; we have assumed the adoption of a dome as the great feature of the modern cathedral, because it is the grandest possible form in architecture capable of far more than has yet been done with it, and is the natural and obvious manner of roofing, in a monumental form, a central area such as we have been regarding as the essential element of the modern cathedral plan.

Eventually the insistence on Gothic was quietly dropped, as, despite previous declarations to the contrary, designs poured in – 103 by June 1902, to be assessed by G.F. Bodley and Richard Norman Shaw. Bodley was now an old man; born in 1827, he was one of the survivors of the great age of Gothic Revivalism. The two men had to spend a great deal of time on the project, and in October issued their report. Having stated that the new Cathedral should be a stately, a dignified and a beautiful building which, as they said, was obvious, they went on to look for a 'design having a distinctive character of its own, and one not without originality'. Under the unsurprising heading of 'Gothic pre-eminent', they elaborated:

> We were prepared to find more designs of a Renaissance or a Classical manner. We were surprised to find so few in those styles, and those, we feel bound to say, not commanding nor remarkable. The main body of the best designs sent in are Gothic. This seemed to point to Gothic as the style from which we should find it practical to select. And, indeed, that manner is accepted by most as generally the suitable one, except under special circumstances, for church-building. In making a selection there seemed no doubt but that our own English phase of the style should be adhered to.

The reaction of most architects can easily be guessed, but some at least must have been pleased. In any event, five entries qualified their designers for the final selection: Austin & Paley, C.A. Nicholson, Giles Gilbert Scott, Malcolm Stark and W.J. Tapper – all, it goes without saying, Gothic designs. A further eight schemes were selected for an honourable mention: Sir Thomas Drew, J. Oldrid Scott, A.H. Skipworth, H.C. Corlette, C.A. Nicholson, F. Walley, James H. Cook, Reilly & Peach. Designs by all five finalists were submitted by April 1903 and in June the decision was announced; Bodley and Shaw chose the design of the 21-year-old Catholic G.G. Scott, only to find their decision rather unwelcome in a determinedly Protestant city and the Committee decided not to accept any of the designs. The upheaval did not ruffle the selectors' enthusiasm for their task or for their choice:

PLATE XV
PLATE XVI
PLATE XVII
PLATE XVIII

> What we had to find was not the best or the most beautiful drawings, but the best idea and the finest conception. We had to look at the real effect of the building rising to its final completion, at the dimensions and proportions of the different parts, we had to look for a fine and a noble proportion, combined with an evident knowledge of detail. Lastly, we had to look for that power, combined with beauty that makes a great and

noble building. In the set of drawings marked No. 1 we find these qualities pre-eminently shown. Mr. Scott's design shows a cathedral of a total length of about 480 ft and an extreme width of 200 ft.

But while they praised Scott irrespective of the consequences, *The Builder's Journal*, keen-eyed, surveyed the general press response to the impasse:

> Outside opinions on architectural matters are often interesting, sometimes valuable. "Truth" says:– Architects of position are not likely to trouble themselves further with the work of a Committee of dunderhead amateurs which proceeds in so eccentric and skimble-skamble a fashion. The building of Liverpool Cathedral is, *a priori*, a hideous waste of money, and the egregious Committee need not be so feverishly anxious to provide for a large congregation, considering the notorious fact that not a church in the city is ever more than half full, and most of them are nearly empty at all the services. "The Globe" says:– The result of the competition . . . is, to say the least, extremely disappointing . . . Liverpool is, therefore, as far as ever from obtaining a cathedral which will do it credit; "The Tablet" says:– This very suggestion that the pulpit is the most important feature of a cathedral reminds us that Liverpool retains its reputation as a city of stalwart Protestantism. When we go on to add that Mr. Giles Gilbert Scott is a Catholic, perhaps a further clue may be supplied as to the attitude of some of the people of Liverpool towards his design . . . When Mr. Coventry Patmore built the Church of Our Lady Star of the Sea at Hastings he employed a Protestant architect of great repute, Mr. Basil Champneys. One thing is obvious: if a Catholic is to be debarred from employment in the building of a Protestant cathedral, the invitation to competitors should notify this restriction. It should be frankly stated at the outset that no Catholics need apply. The Liverpool Cathedral competition has been, from its initiation, about as unsatisfactory as it possibly could be, but it may have served a useful purpose if it should offer a wholesome warning to architects and prove a check to the growth of practices in the conduct of architectural competitions which cannot be too strongly condemned.

But while a solution to the muddle was sought, it was at least possible to consider the design, on exhibition to the public like those for the first competition. Scott's was surprisingly well received:

> Of the five designs submitted we cordially endorse the advisory architects' selection of No. 1 as the one best worked out, showing greatest interest and originality, and suggesting the most scholarly yet restrained detail. As traditional Gothic Revivalist work this design has merit; but what we should like to see would be equal knowledge lines, to the solution of the problem of a cathedral built in present times and entirely suited to modern needs.

Austin and Paley fared less well:

> The grouping of the two transept towers and of the central tower and dome does not strike us as happy and

well-balanced. In the detail there is great monotony and a want of effective proportion . . . In this design, we see exemplified the unsatisfactory note of all the designs, an ill-digested magnifying of parish church work and the re-hashing-up of familiar mediaeval forms. In particular the juxtaposition of coarse detail in the lower stages of the central tower with the more attenuated detail adjacent, as though there had been, owing to the size of the building, an exhaustion of the records of precedent.

Stark's and Tapper's schemes did not please *The Builder's Journal* as the following comments show:

This design is a further illustration of that which we should like to see the end of: the busy reproduction of mediaeval forms. This is the twentieth century and not the fourteenth; but were this design carried out, and mellowed by time, it might be difficult to say whether the fabric were a nineteenth-century "restoration" of some mediaeval cathedral, or a full-sized model of old work.

The author of this design appears to have endeavoured to adapt to the purposes of a cathedral the plan of a wide nave and narrow aisles frequently seen in modern parish churches. The result is a large unimpeded area for the congregation, but in so large a building those at the end of the nave would not be well placed for hearing the preacher, if that is a *sine qua non* for a cathedral.

Finally, Nicholson, in the view of *The Builder* showed:

A very clever and original treatment of the plan; it may perhaps suffer under the accusation of being rather too clever. We noticed the sketch design for this, in our review of the first competition, as an able but somewhat eccentric one. The design as a whole is exceedingly original, and though we should not have recommended its adoption, as being too restless and deficient in simplicity of motif, it will always rank as a credit to its author . . . who then had to see things from the Committee's point of view. . . . If we put ourselves in the place of the Committee, who are apparently old-fashioned churchmen with old-fashioned ideas about church architecture, it must be admitted that in Mr. Scott's design thay have got what is, on the whole, a fine expression of the kind of cathedral architecture they want; and one cannot but be pleased and interested to see the good old name of Gilbert Scott rising again into architectural prominence in the third generation. What we regret is that, if this cathedral is built, the century will hardly be half out before it will be regarded as an anachronism.

There was eventually a peaceful settlement of the issue of the winner. The Committee agreed to accept Scott, supervised by Bodley, a fact reported with world-weary sadness by *The Builder* as it surveyed the history of the competition:

Considering that Mr. Scott is a young man, and has not hitherto carried out any large work, it does not seem unreasonable that they should wish to have the co-operation of an older and well-known church architect; but we must say that it is an unusual proceeding, and a bad precedent, to make one of the assessors in a competition a partner in carrying out the work, unless indeed Mr. Bodley's position is to be that of a friendly adviser only. The whole competition, in fact, has been mismanaged from first to last, both in the choice of site and in the conduct of the competition. Two or three of the finest designs, by men of notable talent, were passed over in the first competition, while honourable mentions were accorded to designs far inferior; and in the final choice the assessors seem to have entirely ignored the special requirements of the Committee, and have thereby nearly wrecked the competition. The Committee, though apparently not very decided in the main as to what they wanted, were clear upon one point; they wished to have a large central space on the plan, on which a large congregation could be collected within hearing of a preacher. The assessors have awarded the first prize to a design which entirely ignores this requirement. It is not a creditable result.

The decision was not altogether a pleasing one, but at least the winner was assured of some chance of building his cathedral. Meanwhile the architects themselves issued their views. Austin and Paley's report was sober, devoid of the eulogies of previous competitions. Malcolm Stark, equally logical, tackled the issue of the inescapable open space and the church's style:

The style of the cathedral has advisedly been left to the competitors. The author of this design has adopted the Gothic style, believing, as he does, that it is more suitable than any other for the full and perfect expression of ecclesiastical purposes. Two distinct types appeal to the author; these are the Early English, with its dignified simplicity of outline, and that type of Gothic which prevailed during the reign of Edward III. Internally, the design may be said to be a concession to precedent. In the treatment of the nave, aisles, and transepts a simple and conservative character is maintained.

Tapper anxiously verified the height of his church:

The nave having a span of 76 ft demands a proportionate height, and this has been made two to one, the same as at King's College Chapel, Cambridge, only on a much larger scale, the height from floor to apex of vault being 152ft. Lest this should be thought extravagant, it might be well to mention that buildings of such dimensions exist in quiet small towns, such as Beauvais, Amiens, Gerona, and many others, small, indeed, as compared with the great City of Liverpool. The great width of the nave does not permit comparison with any of the English cathedrals.

Nicholson wrote most fulsomely of all, on matters both elevated and mundane, sometimes with just a hint of pique:

In view of the fact that large unobstructed areas have been successfully enclosed by the builders of Sta. Sophia, of Gerona, of Ely, of Florence, and of St. Paul's cathedrals, it was felt that it would be a confession of incompetence to shirk the constructive and artistic difficulties of the problem set by the Cathedral Committee and their assessors. The principal effect aimed at internally was a contrast between the sober and massive nave and the open and brightly lighted crossing. This treatment was adopted with the purpose of avoiding a gloomy and confined effect like that of the sanctuary of St. Paul's. A crypt, under the chapterhouse, is intended to contain a second heating-chamber and a storeroom for bicycles, with entrance to St. James's Road. The chief difficulty in the design of the exterior has been the treatment of the central tower. Its diameter being very great, and the length of the cathedral being expressly limited to 450 ft, in order to bring it as far as possible into scale with its surroundings its plan approaches nearly to a circle, and the tower proper is crowned with a small lantern, sufficiently large to take its place in the general grouping of the cathedral as seen from the high ground of Hope-Street, or from distant points of view. The design of this tower is felt to be crude in many respects, but a satisfactory solution of so difficult a problem could hardly have been arrived at in the six months or so in which competitors were expected to mature their ideas. In so large a church special provision has to be made for access to roofs, gutters, and windows, for purposes of inspection, cleansing, and repairs; convenient stores must be arranged for scaffolding materials and the like; the best positions must be found for heating-chambers, lavatories, cloakrooms, and housemaid's cupboards, all of which details, though not apparent upon the surface, are yet very essential to the durability and comfort of the building. The design was intended to be executed in incombustible materials with concrete external roofs, double roofs being considered necessary in the English climate.

Not only did the finalists have much to say, others too wanted to comment. Such continued interest was not at all surprising: it was, after all, the great competition of the age in England. H.C. Corlette, honourably mentioned, produced a design of which he wrote:

> It was intended in contriving this plan of a cathedral that by its internal arrangement and external composition it should express the facts of which it should be a visible symbol. It was to show the relative importance of the several parts of the building . . .'

Reilly and Peach's idealised scheme was admitted as such from

> They do not represent a scheme for a building to be erected on the St. James's Mount or any particular site, but rather a design embodying what, in the author's opinion, were the essential features of an ideal modern cathedral. These seemed to be, firstly, a monumental building; secondly, one in which a large congregation could worship; and thirdly, a *campo santo* for the burial of the illustrious dead. The Greek cross plan was chosen because it offers a great opportunity for obtaining a monumental pile.

PLATE XIX

Nor was excitement, virtuosity and the occasional quirk restricted to those singled out for praise. To choose just three of the others, A. Beresford Pite, W.R. Lethaby and C.R. Mackintosh all produced churches of a wayward, isolationist genius: Pite's, a stunning Byzantine pile of the greatest sophistication; Lethaby's, a huge low mass of flagrant modernism

when compared to the more sedate schemes. Any of the three would have added an irrepressible individualism to Liverpool, would have given the city an emblem round which the fires of debate might, if not roar as flames, at least smoulder continuously.

Instead Liverpool had, with some ill-grace and after some considerable prevarication, chosen itself a Gothic church. A lost opportunity, thought some. A chance for a triumph, thought others, and they were right. Bodley and Scott, well chosen according to the official history of the cathedral as joint architects (ultimately, with the instinct for compromise which is the Englishman's outstanding characteristic, the Committee decided to invite Mr. Bodley to act as joint architect with Mr. Scott) were instructed to submit plans for the east end foundation by October 1903, and on July 19th 1904, the foundation stone was laid by King Edward VII and Queen Alexandra, in a crowded amphitheatre erected for the occasion, allowing work to press ahead on the Lady Chapel. From 1907 onwards, after the death of Bodley, Scott was sole architect, and he exercised his freedom two years later, when he proposed radical changes, replacing his two towers by one massive central tower, and the shortening of the nave from six bays to three. This involved the abandoning of some work already completed, and took the Committee a year to deliberate upon, but in 1910, it was accepted, giving us the cathedral that now is completed.

116 The interior of Brooks's Cathedral, designed to accommodate the largest possible congregation. For special occasions, the triforium gallery could provide space for several thousand people. As with the exterior, the style inside, with its four-storey elevation, was typically French.

114 H. W. Brewer's individual response to the concept of a Cathedral in Liverpool. Commissioned by *The Builder* in 1885, his view shows a restored Notre Dame in Paris, transported to Liverpool and framed by the classical colonnades of St. George's Hall. (see page 110)

115 Liverpool Cathedral: James Brooks's design from *The Building News*, February 19th, 1886. He chose the early High Gothic style, and with its ambulatory, flying buttresses, large rose window and west spires derived from Chartres, his Cathedral is entirely un-English. This perspective shows how close the 1886 site was to the classical bulk of St. George's Hall.

LIVERPOOL CATHEDRAL COMPETITION.
DESIGN SUBMITTED BY Mr JAMES BROOKS F.R.I.B.A. ARCHT
VIEW FROM THE NORTH EAST SHOWING RELATIVE POSITIONS OF THE CATHEDRAL AND St GEORGES HALL.

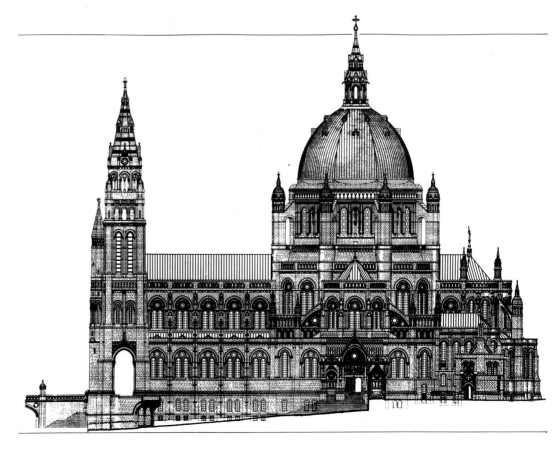

117 'We think that no trouble or expense ought to be spared in order to make this present work as great a success as Sir Christopher Wren's noble church . . . The style we have chosen . . . is of strictly English character.' Bodley and Garner's design from the west, demonstrating their love of fourteenth-century architecture which they thought appropriate to 'this (church) which will be the most important ecclesiastical building that has been planned for many generations in England'.

118 1886's winner: G. W. Emerson was the most persuasive of all the competitors, submitting a vast and reasoned tract with his design. Here, he shows his addiction to the use of the dome 'because its mass, in combination with its height, gives the greatest attainable grandeur and impressiveness'.

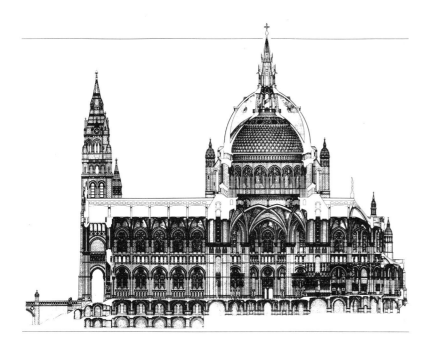

119 A longitudinal section of Emerson's cathedral. Despite the proximity of St. George's Hall, Emerson chose Gothic. Classical architecture was 'pagan and un-English in origin, while Gothic is Christian and more our national style'. It would be hard to find any English antecedent for his particular reinterpretation of his chosen style.

120 Emerson's cathedral, in its intended setting.

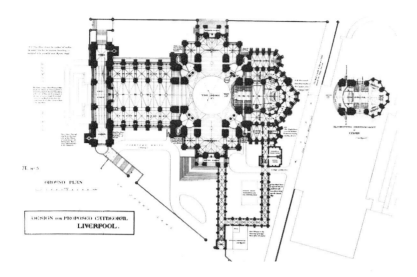

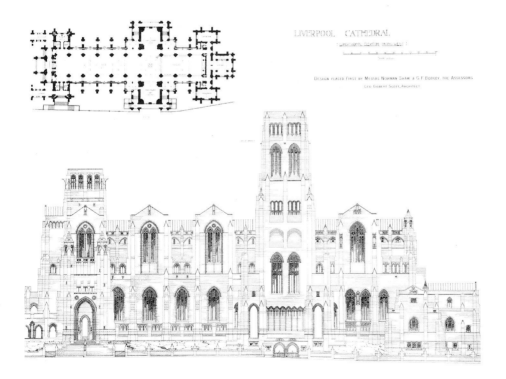

121 Emerson's ground plan. Like other competitors, Emerson intended, for liturgical reasons, to have a large central space so that 'nearly 1400 persons can be accommodated in an unbroken area within 100 feet of the pulpit'.

122 The interior of Emerson's dome, which its author considered to be an improvement on Wren's St. Paul's, and which, he claimed, had an affinity to the 'beautiful Mohammedan domes so common in the East which are practically Gothic'.

123 Liverpool's second competition of 1902 was won by Giles Gilbert Scott, aged only twenty-two. His winning design pleased the judges because it had 'that power, combined with beauty that makes a great and noble building'. Scott's Cathedral was 480 feet long and 200 feet across at its widest part.

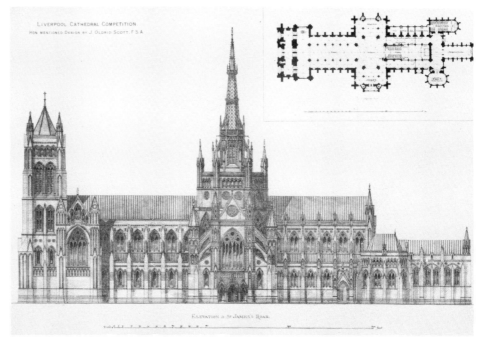

124 Cross section of the transepts of G. G. Scott's design, which were subsequently altered.

125 J. Oldrid Scott's spired cathedral for the Liverpool competition.

126 'Able but somewhat eccentric'. C. A. Nicholson's use of an octagonal drum-like central lantern was determinedly original, but rather alarmed *The Builder:* 'we should not have recommended its adoption, as being too restless and deficient in simplicity of motif . . .'

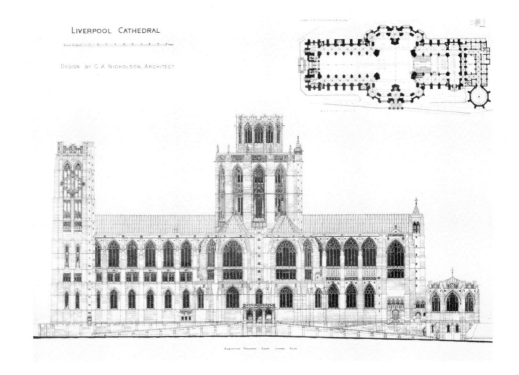

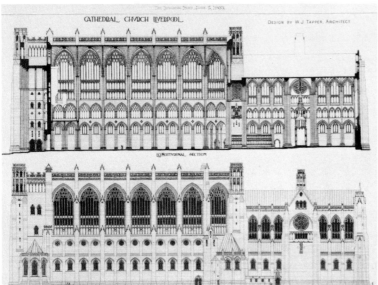

127 Austin and Paley's design for the 1902
competition was criticised in the
architectural press for its 'great monotony
and want of effective proportion'. 'In this
design we see exemplified an ill digested
magnifying of parish church work and the
rehashing up of familiarly medieval forms.'

128 Malcolm Stark's scheme of 1902 with a
spire inspired by that of St. Michael's in
Coventry.

129 Extreme internal height characterised
Tapper's longitudinal section, together with
sophisticated handling of tracery in the
immense windows.

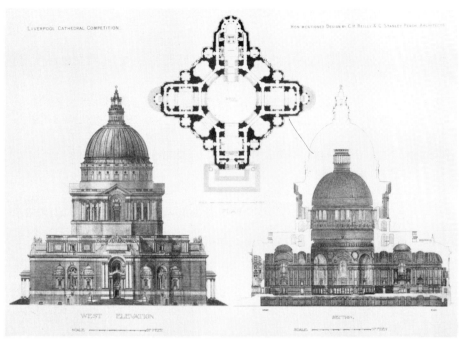

131 Reilly and Peach proposed this severe classical interior for Liverpool.

130 'The essential features of a modern cathedral.' Reilly and Peach's design was not intended for the Liverpool competition but was prompted by the furore that that event caused amongst architects. Bravely, their ideal was not a Gothic, but a classical church.

132 Severity and verticality: Skipworth's scheme rises from a base of polychromatic stonework through great expanses of unadorned stonework to its western towers. More obviously modern than many other competitors, it did not get through to the initial selection.

133 Byzantine sophistication: A. Beresford Pite's cathedral was a complex, magnificent reinterpretation of Sta. Sophia, but was not in a style likely to have appealed to the judges.

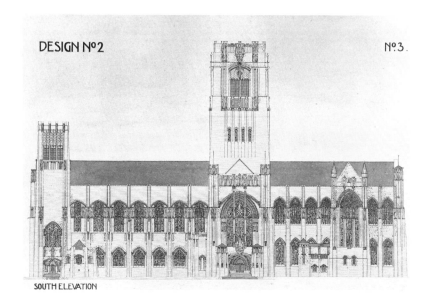

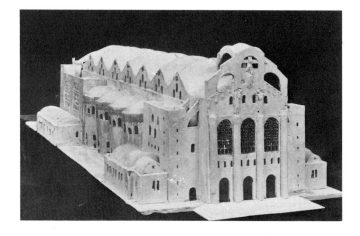

134 Mackintosh, Scottish genius of the Arts and Crafts movement, produced a design which, had it been built, would have been the largest church that movement created. Particularly noteworthy is the tracery of the transept window, a combination of sinuousness and severe verticality.

135 Breaking with tradition: W. R. Lethaby's concrete church was a complete contrast to the traditional entries for Liverpool. Lethaby considered that concrete allowed more dignified planning, as well as more substantial superstructures.

136 The foundation stone of the cathedral laid by King Edward VII and Queen Alexandra in 1904.

137 The cathedral from the south in the 1930s, by which time the Lady Chapel was completed and work was well under way on the bulk of the transepts and central tower.

138 The cathedral from the north-east. The great change from Scott's winning design was the replacement of his two transept towers by a more massive single central tower, rising from pairs of smaller transepts.

139 The architect, Giles Gilbert Scott.

11. SIR EDWIN LUTYENS – THE LAST GREAT ENDEAVOUR

*N*ever before or since has an architect's reputation soared, plummeted and risen again with such speed as that of Sir Edwin Lutyens. At his death in 1944, architects, patrons and innumerable friends concurred that the twentieth-century colossus of English architecture had left a legacy of houses, governmental buildings and so on which was quite unsurpassed. He had recaptured in his country houses the subtleties of Georgian and Tudor in such a sublime way that these revived arts were unaware of this most gentle of captivities. Compelled to choose but one of the qualities that make these works so immediately classic, it would be the air of tumbled formality, the effortless combination of dignity of architectural form with the right degree of marshalled abandon in the setting of their gardens.

1944 was a time for yearning for the tranquility of the English past, and those writing to appraise Lutyens at his passing could of course draw on his architecture. But equally laudatory were celebrations of Lutyens the man; Harold Nicolson's later judgement, that never since the days of Sheridan and Goldsmith had a man of genius been so widely beloved, was entirely apt. Lutyens was a universal man, universal in the variety of talents that he possessed; more rare, was the universality of affection that he felt for others, and that he inspired in return.

That this quiet man should be quietly dispatched to a pantheon of neglect through the 1950s and 1960s seems already extraordinary. But it is only in the past ten years that his rehabilitation has been effected. Although it is impossible to gauge the effect of unbuilt projects on an architect's reputation, the continuing importance of Lutyens's work would have remained in the public eye had the most majestic of all his designs been realized – that for the Roman Catholic cathedral in Liverpool.

Lutyens is now fêted for country houses and far flung imperial building on the grandest scale: his houses held by many to be the last word in the tradition of superb classical building. If his domed cathedral had risen in Liverpool on the monumental crypt that so auspiciously started the project, Lutyens would have given us the one twentieth-century classical building to combine stateliness with architectural bravado of the surest kind.

Liverpool was not the first great cathedral that Lutyens conceived. The original intentions for the imperial capital of New Delhi, India, included not only broad avenues, the vast Viceroy's house, the barracks, stables and other myriad ancillary buildings that were built, but also a cathedral. Indicative of the extent of Britain's history of cultural domination in India, the idea of a cathedral struck many as the explicit symbol of the link between the Church and the State. The religious Englishman was, according to Sir George Birchwood, a figure who commanded the highest respect amongst Indians. A cathedral would celebrate the religious fortitude, the strength of moral character of the British and most of all would symbolise God's succour and guidance to the British in the trials and mis-adventures of the Indian mutiny.

Men with such a nineteenth-century view of recent history naturally held out for a nineteenth-century style of church. Unaware both of the furore and of the importance of the arguments that flowed so acidly around the Liverpool Anglican cathedral competition, (as described in the preceding chapter) they wanted for New Delhi a Gothic spired cathedral, a Revivalist finger of pious admonition to the populace. It was not a view that appealed to Lutyens. He pointed out that large Gothic windows would produce a very oppressive interior in a land of unrelenting heat. He also declined to give such an outmoded conception of a cathedral the prominence his opponents felt it deserved, threatening to ostracize the church to a site lacking dignity on the periphery of New Delhi.

That was 1912: in 1917 the opportunity arose to build a cathedral more to his taste. Untramelled by the ramblings of ageing Indian civil servants and their desires for an oppressive Gothic oven, Lutyens began to conceive a centrally planned church with three arms, oversailed by a large dome on a comparatively plain drum. This at once set up a sense of movement and excitement in the exterior. Long walls radiated away from the cone of the church at wide angles. It was a very engaging, Mannerist manipulation of mathematics, given cohesion and literally weight, by the mass of the dome above.

This was no mere architectural caprice. Lutyens always had the function of his scheme in mind. In one of the three arms he intended choir stalls, a Lady chapel and chapter house; a second held the library and baptistry; while in the third, appropriately for New Delhi, chapels for the chivalric orders of the Star of India and Indian Empire – chapels where Church and State met in ecclesiastical pageantry.

The central space under the dome provided the greatest opportunity for sophisticated planning. The three angles were used as the site for the Viceroy's tribune, a lectern and a pulpit. The high altar was to be directly opposite the Viceroy's tribune. The plan had the clarity and simplicity that seemed to make it, like all great architecture, the obvious solution, at once audacious and in keeping with its traditional function.

The exterior too was individual yet in harmony with the Viceroy's residence, topped appropriately by a slender cross, determined and elegantly Christian in an otherwise unchristian and secular setting. The rapidly sketched details confirmed Lutyens's mastery of the domed form: comparatively simple large elements adorned the walls, providing a stately uncluttered, classical punctuation for the church's grand statement. Tall columns and large arches framed the entrance, four great square windows rose above it. Horizontal strength was expressed by the weight of the entablature, and by the support that the drum gave the dome, but was not so prominent as to undermine the rising cupola leading to the cross.

Given the importance of the cathedral to the imperial character which New Delhi was to have, it would have been safe to assume that funds would be forthcoming. But this was a false assumption and by 1923 it was distressingly clear that only something rather less than Lutyens's original church would be feasible. A traditional solution was sought: it was decided to have a competition. Lutyens had the slight compensation of being sole assessor, but leafing through the responses of others to the brief that had once so challenged his own talents cannot have been the most cheering of experiences. Nonetheless he came to a decision, selecting Henry Medd's calm and very English design which reflected a more muted side of Lutyens's late seventeenth-century style. Medd's church was a very satisfying design of attractively massed forms. But necessarily, the grandeur and resonance of Lutyens's scheme were no longer possible.

From the disappointment of New Delhi, Lutyens turned to another cathedral, one which promised to be the most impressive church ever built in Britain. Liverpool had, after two competitions, after the endeavours of hundreds of architects and after the dismay and disapproval of the press at large, managed to settle upon an Anglican cathedral of undisputed majesty. By the mid-1920s it was already a large, crane-bedecked bulk rising visibly on its St. James's Mount site. But Liverpool was equally important as a centre of English Catholicism. In the Anglican church Liverpool was a mere diocese, whereas in the Roman church it was archdiocese, and one which had in Richard Downey an archbishop of great vision. Appointed in 1928, Downey at once began to instigate plans for a suitable cathedral. After all, in an arch-diocese founded in 1850 the lack of a cathedral of opposite dignity was a major fault. The ineffectual attempts at a new cathedral, the Church of Our Lady Immaculate, were unfinished and hardly fitting. It was time for a new start on a new site.

The new site was quickly found: Brownlow Hill, close to the university, offered an eminence that would parallel the marvellous siting of the rival Anglican cathedral by Scott. That cathedral was Gothic, and the result of a competition. Dr. Downey's would be neither. Instead he approached Lutyens, with whom he had had slight acquaintance and invited him to Liverpool to discuss the church he intended to build there. This was no time for reticence, and reticence was the last word one could apply to Lutyens's immediate ideas, which were initiated in secrecy.

It was a commission to which Lutyens was deeply attached:

Lutyens in good form . . . He is thrilled with the prospects of building the new R.C. cathedral for Liverpool, a church bigger than Scott's, better sited, more dramatic, more beautiful. He has a hundred fantasies about it, how to arrange the holy water stoops, how to design liveries for the sacristan (he asked to borrow our papal guard's uniform) – how to do this that and the other in some fashion which will be new as well as canonical, picturesque as well as conventional. He certainly is full of witty fantasies and must amuse even if he doesn't sometimes alarm the portly Archbishop.

wrote the tenth Earl of Balcarres in his diary for October 1930. Since the Archbishop was as ebullient a character as his architect, theirs must have been an unusually happy relationship, cemented from the first by Downey's offering Lutyens a cocktail on the architect's arrival in Liverpool. Both shared the joy of the project; and the Archbishop must have felt at least some inspiration from his architect when he spoke at the service to celebrate the acquisition of the site. *The Architects' Journal* reported it fulsomely on 3rd September 1930:

Addressing an open-air service of thanksgiving for the securing of the site, held in Thingwall Park, Liverpool, on Sunday last, the Archbishop of Liverpool said the site would compare even with the ideal spots chosen for the renowned Gothic cathedrals of that golden period of Catholicism, the twelfth and thirteenth centuries. The cathedral which they proposed to build was not something designed to meet merely the spiritual requirements of that great city, nor even merely those wider needs of the teeming Archdiocese of Liverpool – it was to be the Metropolitan Cathedral of the North of England, the rallying point for the Archdiocese of Liverpool, with its Suffragan Sees of Leeds, Middlesborough, Hexham and Newcastle, Lancaster and Salford. It was to be to them what York Minster was to their forefathers. It was to make Liverpool a great ecclesiastical centre like Rheims or Cologne, where men of all nations might unite under one roof, in one common worship.

Lutyens's cathedral surpassed mere superlatives. Grander than any church with the exception of St. Peter's in Rome, it was a pink and grey citadel of faith, a renaissance of Mont St. Michel in which the rock as well as its crown was an integral part of the great church. Like New Delhi, Liverpool according to Lutyens was to be a city of the dome throughout, and the architect determined to surpass both that of St. Peter's, disparagingly referred to as 'that pimple' and that of his adored St. Paul's, London. At Liverpool the dome was to be 510 feet high – 60 feet above St. Peter's, more than 130 feet taller than St. Paul's. Its diameter was to be 168 feet, easily larger than the 137 feet of St. Peter's and the 112 feet of St. Paul's. A splendid model, displayed in 1934, gave an accurate and thrilling vision of the exterior. As for its cavernous interior, Christopher Hussey in his masterful life of the architect, commented that 'The interior combines the dark and lofty mystery of Notre Dame with the amplitude of Sta. Sophia beneath the dome'. Both the design and the decision to build the church called forth acclaim with subtle aptness from the architect of a commended domed design for the Anglican cathedral, C.H. Reilly, who appraised Lutyens in *Country Life*:

PLATE
XX

Even in this cathedral-building age, for such it really is, with Sir Giles Scott's great building rising rapidly in Liverpool, Bentley's magnificent interior for all to see at Westminster, and now a cathedral projected at Guildford, not to mention the three or four building at the present moment in America – it is, nevertheless, an arresting fact that Liverpool, certainly not at the most flourishing epoch in her career, should be starting to build another and much greater one. What, however, is more important to architects and to all who love architecture is that this great opportunity, the greatest that can come to any designer, has fallen to Sir Edwin Lutyens. What would the man who has led English architecture for so many years, first in the domestic field, then in his great town plan and palace at Delhi, and more recently in banks, blocks of offices and flats all over London, do when presented with the highest of all that appeals to the imagination? There are none of the muddles Wren got into trying to bring up to the same level eight arches over openings of different widths. Indeed, Sir Edwin here obtains both the simplicity and majesty of St. Peter's with the romance and interest of the long vistas of St. Paul's. The materials suggested for the exterior are stainless steel plates for the dome and long Roman-shaped bricks two or three feet long and an inch to two inches thick for the main walling. If these bricks cannot be made locally they could, perhaps, be brought from Rome, where they are still being made outside the city, coming down the Tiber in barges and up the Mersey at no great cost. The estimated cost of the cathedral is three million pounds, but a quarter of a million is already in sight, while the poor of Liverpool are subscribing at the rate of a thousand pounds a month.

He pinpointed not only the scale of the church but the discipline with which it was made a controlled and a peaceful whole: he admired the grouping of the nave and aisle piers into pairs, which allowed Lutyens to run his cross-vault from side to side of the cathedral at different levels, lighting the higher over the lower. This freed the exterior from the 'worry' of myriad windows, and gave sophisticated interior lighting effects. Unity was given by the repetition of arches of the same proportion, large and small. Its vaulting too was controlled by Roman vaults of 'definitely connected proportions'.

The exterior, freer in treatment than the interior was dominated by the triple arches of the main entrance. Here, Reilly was reminded of Lutyens's 'great memorial to the Unknown Dead at Arras':

> Living near the site, I feel these great arches will look down over the town with immense effect, while their deep shadows and those of the recesses above the two side ones will make a very strongly and very effectively modelled front.

The foundation stone of the church was laid at Whitsuntide, 1933. Lutyens designed an elegant canopy specially for the occasion. The church itself would take up 5 acres of its 9¼ acre site, and by 1938 work had progressed on the crypt to the extent that masses had already taken place within it. The crypt was

built almost entirely of blue bricks from St. Helen's, highlighted by dressings of Cornish granite. The walls of the Chapel of Relics had by then been lined with two types of travertine – a golden one from Austria, and a cream one from Italy. *The Builder*, reporting in 1938, said that 2,000,000 bricks had already been used by the 60 workmen employed on the site. 'The next stage' it confidently asserted 'in the development of the cathedral will be the construction of the Sanctuary floor and of the Sanctuary itself. The dome and transept will follow'.

In 1938 there seemed no reason why this should not be the case, despite the comparative poverty of the city and the huge cost of the church. At first even the Second World War did not interrupt the work; a further two million bricks were used. But by 1941 the intensity of the conflict, and especially the punishment Liverpool received from the air, had halted the project. The unfinished crypt, in many places open to weather damage, then functioned as an air-raid shelter. Immediately after the war, Liverpool faced such enormous problems that the church could not be recommenced. By the mid-1950s, the estimated cost had increased to £27 million. The original scheme was out of the question. A small domed cathedral by Adrian Gilbert Scott was considered but rapidly abandoned as well, and in 1959 Cardinal Heenan announced a competition for a wholly new design, giving us the cathedral of Sir Frederick Gibberd.

Christopher Hussey called Lutyens's church 'infinitely the largest, most original, and most perfectly integrated church ever to have been projected as a homogenous whole by a single architect'. A study of the model, and perspectives show the grounds on which he made this statement.

Finally, a Lutyens coda. In 1942 he proposed a narthex for Westminster Abbey, which he exhibited at the Royal Academy in 1943. It was not a design which had much hope of progressing beyond being an intriguing idea, but it shows on a small scale, the same mastery of centralised planning, and of exterior massing that so characterised his two stillborn cathedrals. At Westminster a square ground-plan contained an octagonal space with square chambers radiating into the aisles. Its exterior was unified by a low pyramidal roof, not dissimilar to that on the chapter house of Llandaff Cathedral. It was perhaps a caprice by a genius at the end of his life, but one where the sum of his achievement, albeit in miniature, quietly presented itself.

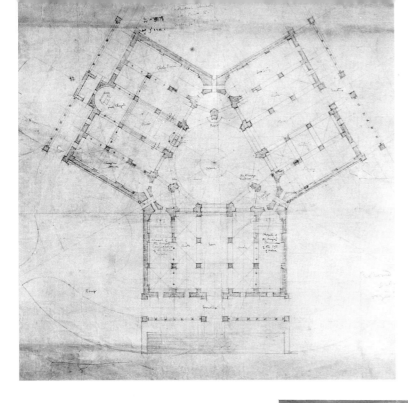

140 Portrait of Sir Edwin Lutyens by R. Lutyens, capturing the humour of the great architect.

141 Lutyens's three-armed ground plan for the cathedral at New Delhi. The Viceroy's tribune and pulpit face each other across an angle of the central dome; one of the two naves is flanked by the library and baptistry, the choir by choir rooms and the chapter house. Lutyens included both the liturgical parts of the church and its anciliary buildings in one concept.

142 Sketch elevations of the cathedral for New Delhi. The dome echoes that on the Viceroy's residence. The lower sketch shows how the dome would relate to the three arms of the church.

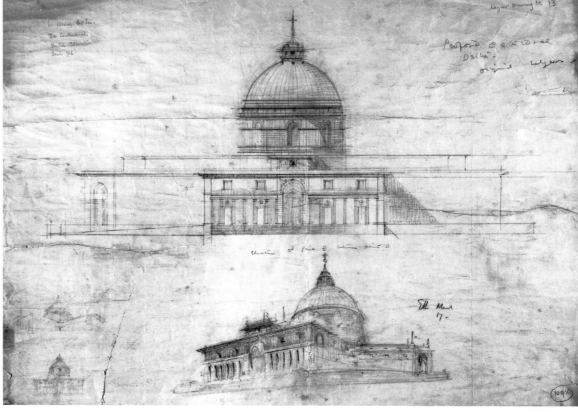

LIVERPOOL METROPOLITAN CATHEDRAL

EAST ELEVATION

NORTH ELEVATION

144 Liverpool Metropolitan Cathedral, north
elevation. From its inception Lutyens's
design was intended to be the last word in
ecclesiastical grandeur. Its dome alone was
510 feet high, 130 feet taller than that of St.
Paul's.

143 The cathedral from the east, showing the
campanili. (see page 124)

LIVERPOOL METROPOLITAN CATHEDRAL

WEST ELEVATION

145 The west elevation of Liverpool
Metropolitan Cathedral, with the façade
topped by a statue of Christ. (see page 126)

146 Lutyens designed the canopy for the
ceremony of laying the foundation stone.

147 The plan and elevation of the narthex that
Lutyens proposed for Westminster Abbey.

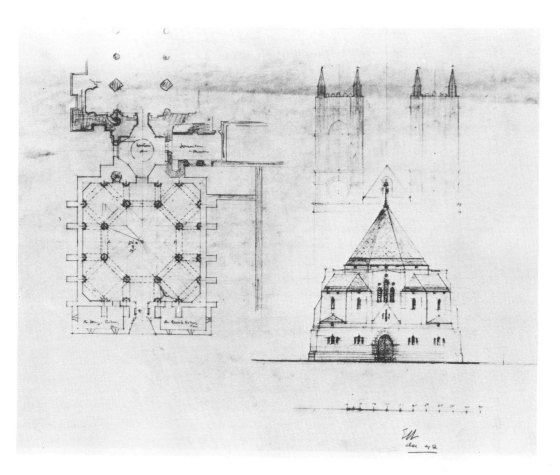

12. COLOGNE AND OTHER COMPLETIONS

*T*hus far, we have looked at the schemes which foundered, where the original design was discarded through the vagaries of fate in the form of poverty, pestilence, war and perhaps most deadly of all, inertia. Milan shows how one church can go through centuries of artistic endeavour to end with a half-hearted mixture of a façade; St. Peter's, Rome, changed as each decade contributed its idea of perfection to that most prestigious of projects. It might seem that it is inevitable for a major church to be altered or mutilated as time passes and thus remain incomplete.

There are a few heartening exceptions to this rule of which Cologne Cathedral is a marvellous example. Cologne, seat of one of the most affluent and influential Rhenish princely Archbishops, was a trading city of immense wealth and importance in the Middle Ages. In the thirteenth century, the ascendancy of French High Gothic architecture made many in Europe wish to emulate it. At Cologne this was attempted under the episcopacy of Konrad von Hochstaden, whose skills in organisation and management meant that the mammoth undertaking of a new cathedral could have a stable financial basis. In 1248 work began on the choir, which in authentic French manner, had ambulatory and radiating chapels. The immediate model for the German church was the cathedral at Amiens, and in scale Cologne immediately surpassed it. By the end of the century the full height of the interior had been reached – 141 feet, 40 feet higher than Westminster Abbey and only 15 feet lower than the loftiest of all medieval churches, the brilliant and unstable Beauvais in France. That Cologne should aspire to such magnificence was not only appropriate to the secular standing of the city, but also to the remarkable collection of relics preserved in the church. Its most venerated treasure was the collection relating to the three Magi: in legend they were discovered by Helena, mother of the Emperor Constantine and were brought from their earlier home, Milan, by Frederick Barbarossa, after his conquest of Lombardy in 1164. The rulers of Germany, after their coronation at Aachen, traditionally came to Cologne, to the shrine of the Three Magi to offer gifts. Until the 1240s this ceremony took place in a Carolingian basilican church. The decision to rebuild the cathedral was then partly motivated by the desire to give this ceremony and its focus a majestic setting.

Progress on the building of the church was comparatively speedy. In 1322 the huge choir was consecrated and a temporary wall was constructed to separate it from the transepts and the nave, which were then to be built. About thirty years later, the vast west front was commenced under the architect Michael Parler of the prestigious Parler clan of master-masons, already encountered in

relation to Strasbourg. Initial work was concentrated on the south-west tower, which by 1473 had reached the level of the belfry. Thereafter, unfortunately, a marked decline in the city's fortunes relaxed the work and in 1560 it came to a definite halt. This left the completed choir separated by the hardly commenced nave and transepts from the unequal bulk of the south-west tower and the much more rudimentary north-west one. The unfinished cathedral was a marvel, but a fragmentary one. Inside the choir were, and in places still are, stained glass windows, shrines and ornaments of great refinement. The project had been the object of international praise since its inception. Even Petrarch, who preferred ancient classical architecture to that which was 'modern and ugly' admired it. In Cologne in 1333, he wrote 'in the middle of the city I saw an uncommonly beautiful temple, which, though still incomplete, can be called with good reason, the most magnificent'. In the seventeenth century the cathedral presented an inelegant view to the world. Its most prominent feature was the large wooden crane atop the incomplete south-west tower, a piece of medieval machinery which appears again and again in engravings and views of the city.

Many in Cologne were sure that the cathedral would be completed. One of these was the German Jesuit, Hermann Crombach, born in the city in 1598, who wrote an exhaustive and exhausting account of the cathedral and its saints in 1654, including a chapter on the continuation of the building. It was an optimistic view to hold immediately after the debilitating Thirty Years War, which had ravaged most of Germany and had severely undermined the economy of the independent city states, such as Cologne.

Crombach believed the church would be completed exactly according to its medieval design, all of which survived. This makes an interesting comparison to the fluctuating opinion on a similar and contemporary matter then driving to distraction all concerned with Milan Cathedral. Crombach's tone was in defence of Gothic, but not hysterically so. He took it as read that there was much to commend the style

> The disposition of the whole does not follow the Ionic, Corinthian or Composite Orders, but the Gothic.
>
> However, this does not mean that it is for that reason bad . . . the work is more substantial and the town seems more beautiful, particularly in the exterior aspect . . . Most of the upper ornaments on the buttresses cannot be seen with mortal eyes because of their height . . . (but) he who considers them bad for this reason forgets that the work has been constructed not merely for the admiration of man, but for God.

Crombach went on, at great length, to enumerate the contents of the church and illustrated his piece with an engraving of the design for the west front, apparently at his own expense, presenting this to the city council as an encouragement to continue the building of the towers.

Crombach's allowance of the efficacy of Gothic for Cologne, which veered towards the enthusiastic, was not atypical.

Elsewhere, others were urging the addition of a second Gothic tower at Strasbourg Cathedral. But as the seventeenth century wore on, the German critics of Gothic were as aggressive and audible as those of other nations. Joachim von Sandrart found Gothic foliage carving an abomination:

> Now so thick and numerous as though a whole vineyard were planted on them, now however, so delicate, tenuous and sparse as though they were little cut up pieces of cards.

A dose of acidity acquired from the Italian historian Vasari in conclusion on the origin of Gothic, is a summation of Italian and to a lesser extent, German thought:

> The Goths brought this monstrosity to Italy, for after they had devastated and destroyed Rome and almost all Roman artists had perished in the same wars, they subsequently introduced this vile form of building, whereby they brought upon themselves and pulled down upon their heads more than a thousand million curses throughout all Italy.

This was hardly a healthy time for Gothic to flourish, with vines or without. It could not be expected, despite Crombach's hopeful and generous gift to the city council, that Cologne Cathedral would now be completed. And through most of the eighteenth century, the cathedral languished, visible but abandoned. Then in 1772 a young writer came to Strasbourg and inspired by what he saw there, wrote an essay *Von Deutscher Baukunst* (About German Architecture). In this essay, the young Goethe combined enthusiasm and genius to praise Gothic as it had never been praised before. He criticised the German thinker who deluded himself into denigrating Gothic. Instead of this, he should 'give thanks to God that he can loudly proclaim it German architecture, our architecture, while the Italian can boast none of his own, still less the Frenchman'. This last was a rather unfair and inaccurate swipe but, by then, (the end of his piece) Goethe in his rhetoric was beyond the restraints of mere fact. His Romantic rage in favour of a German Gothic was a revelation for his time. Gothic now had meaning, a pan-Germanic meaning.

Unfortunately, the late eighteenth-century was not the best time for gestures of German national feeling, still less for denigrations of France. Nor was Goethe himself constant in his views on architecture; by 1786, when he visited Italy and saw many examples of classical building, he would write 'this is indeed quite different from our conversing saints, quite different from our pointed small turrets and jagged floral ornaments: thank God I am now rid of them forever!' He was embarrassed by his early enthusiastic views on Gothic and did not want them in a collection of his works.

Nevertheless, Goethe's initial enthusiasm was symptomatic of a rising re-appreciation of Gothic in Europe and in Germany. But it has to be repeated that the last years of the century were hardly propitious for costly Gothic endeavours in architecture. Even while Goethe was in Italy, events in France were leading to the Revolution and the subsequent conquest of most of Germany by the French armies. Cologne, on the Rhine, was immediately both

vulnerable and desirable and was occupied by the invading armies. The cathedral and its treasury were sacked, its rank immediately reduced from the seat of an archbishop to that of a mere parish church, and then the building itself served as a hay store while the contents of its treasury, including the medieval designs for the completion of the Cathedral, were dispersed. It seemed highly unlikely that the drawings could possibly have survived.

Meanwhile other Germans were considering Gothic. Some views were more fascinating than accurate. Schelling, for example, compared Strasbourg to a tree, and since Tacitus, 'as is well known' recorded that Germanic people worshipped their gods beneath trees, Gothic was obviously a German form of building. Less sylvan attempts at appraisal came from Friedrich von Schlegel who toured northern Europe, noting all he saw, such as the 'extreme delicacy . . . beautiful simplicity and pure harmony' of Louvain's city hall. In Cologne he compared the cathedral to a jet of water from a mighty fountain and noted that 'the essence of Gothic consists . . . of the profusion and infiniteness of its inner confirmations.

Whatever conclusions, usually favourable, were reached, the important thing was that Gothic was consistently seizing the imagination of writers in Germany and elsewhere. Gothic cathedrals received more critical attention and more well-ordered praise than at any time since the end of the Middle Ages. Schlegel met similar souls in France, expressly sought out Sulpice Boisserée, who with other enthusiasts for things medieval was taking advantage of the wholesale destruction of monasteries during the French Revolution to acquire medieval art at give-away prices. It was Boisserée who was instrumental in the reawakening of interest in Cologne Cathedral and in communicating this to Goethe, as he had heard that the original design for the cathedral on parchment was in a kitchen in Darmstadt. There it was being used, stretched on a frame, as a rack for drying beans. This culinary fate had somehow saved the drawing. Boisserée transcribed the design and this was soon shown to Goethe. It caused something of a reversal in Goethe's taste: 'With astonishment and silent contemplation one sees the legend of the tower of Babel come true on the banks of the Rhine', he commented. Boisserée's involvement with Cologne continued to be of importance. 1823 saw the publication of his illustrated history of the cathedral. Goethe and Boisserée had been in fairly frequent communication about the cathedral, in 1811, for example, discussing the relative merits of Strasbourg and Cologne. Boisserée's writings were comparatively scientific, patriotic but also intelligent. There were no references to the

French antecedents of the cathedral whatsoever, whereas references to German values were everywhere, to the 'joyous, even ecstatic worship of spring among the Germans'. Similar remarks led to the conclusion that Cologne Cathedral was an innate product of a national spirit, of the German people's spirit. The fact that Boisserée himself was half Belgian and half Italian made this eulogy on things Germanic especially interesting. Boisserée was German by *education;* his mind had been moulded by an acquired view of German nationalism. His writings were symptomatic of German thought at the time. Other Romantics were equally moved by Cologne Cathedral's unfinished state and, as Germany became free of French dominance after Waterloo, a strong movement grew up with German history and German art as two of its central tenets. Cologne Cathedral became an emblem of German history and of German unification, and more and more voices were heard advocating the completion of the church. To aid this Pugin's *True Principles of Pointed or Christian Architecture* was translated into German. This too, pinpointed with great, indeed international, authority, the Christian origins of Gothic architecture. It was one more fact that added to the argument that Cologne Cathedral was the most important building in Germany. The King of Prussia, to whom Cologne had been ceded at Napoleon's fall, became infected with enthusiasm for the project. Finally, in 1842, foundations were laid according to the medieval designs for the incomplete parts of the church and in 1863 the temporary wall separating the choir and nave was demolished, 541 years after it had been built. Seventeen years after that the west towers were completed, again to an original design, reaching 500 feet high. The cathedral was finally consecrated amid scenes that go down in the annals of German history as some of the most fervent and patriotic ever. The original design has been criticised for a lack of balance, for the spikiness of the details, but of greater importance is that it was finally completed after centuries of neglect through which it had seemed improbable that the church would ever be finished. The unexpected and triumphant completion of the Cathedral inspired all who saw it; even the young Jakob Burkhardt, later to chronicle with such enthusiasm the Italian Renaissance, was moved to call it 'a revelation of an unparalleled and divine genius'.

The unforeseen consummation of Cologne is one of the most startling and fascinating examples of the resurgence of abandoned Gothic masterpieces in the nineteenth century, but it is far from being the only one. Of many others, the two great churches in Bristol can be chosen as further examples of the nineteenth-century interest in the restoration of things medieval.

In Bristol, there was not the same tragic history of a city occupied by invading armies, or of immense churches left incomplete because of the poverty of the town. Bristol was instead a victim of the Reformation. In medieval times the Augustinian Abbey in Bristol was the premier church building in the city, with its fourteenth-century hall choir – that is, with the aisles of equal height to the central vessel. Its manipulation of space proved according to Pevsner 'incontrovertibly that English design surpassed that of all countries in the first third of the fourteenth century'. Attached to this choir were fifteenth-century transepts, a low but passable fifteenth-century tower and not much else. The Romanesque nave had been demolished, to be replaced by a sixteenth-century nave the construction of which was under way by 1515. By 1540, its walls had reached the level of the bottom of the window sills; but unfortunately the Dissolution of the Monasteries in that year entirely closed down the building programme. Bristol Abbey was rather more fortunate than its celebrated neighbour Glastonbury, in that it escaped wholesale destruction and was elevated to the rank of cathedral by Henry VIII. This restored pre-eminence was not matched by an attention to the fabric of the church, which for the next three hundred and fifty years was left as a truncated naveless fragment. A naive view, now in the British Museum, shows the imbalance of the mutilated church.

The early nineteenth century was not a time of peace in Bristol: riots in 1831 caused great damage to the chapter house of the cathedral, but at least this attracted attention to the diminutive church. Soon afterwards, the houses which had been built on the site of the nave, right up to the central tower, were removed. A minor restoration of the cathedral took place and the church was reopened in 1840 when the 'frightful Corinthian reredos' was removed. By this time more elaborate plans were afoot. A local artist, Thomas Willson, produced a large watercolour of the cathedral 'as originally intended'. His design, preserved in the Bristol City Art Gallery, was well intentioned but his thought was muddled. The low western towers he suggested for the façade were particularly unfortunate. On the other hand he did appreciate that the nave, to echo the choir, should be a hall church. More serious architects did not consider the problems of Bristol Cathedral until the 1860s when settlement of the central tower necessitated immediate attention. By 1866 the tower's piers had been renovated and the view prevailed that something should be done about a nave. The Dean and the majority of the Chapter proposed a nave of only three bays out of sensible concern for fiscal matters, but it was Canon Morris with his connections in secular Bristol, who suggested seeking the opinion of George Edmund Street.

Street discovered the foundations of the north wall of the nave and proved that the original intention was a nave of six bays. His idea for a new nave were exhibited in Bristol in early 1867 and were accepted in June. His scheme showed a nave consistent with the remaining parts of the medieval church, finished at the west end by twin towers. Although Street died during the building of the nave, it was completed almost to his design by J.L. Pearson, with the result that Bristol now has a cathedral complete in all its parts.

It also has, in St. Mary, Redcliffe, a parish church which had also been left incomplete at the end of the Middle Ages. In this case however it was not the body of the church but its crowning glory, the spire, which had been neglected. Built in the fourteenth century, it was struck by lightning in 1446 and was reduced to a fraction of its former height. It remained, squat and inelegant, until the spirit of restoration which had seized the cathedral authorities also possessed those connected with St. Mary's and in 1872 the spire was restored, four hundred and twenty six years after it had originally been damaged.

Although several centuries separate the abandonment of Bristol's nave, the spire at St. Mary's, and the entire nave and façade at Cologne, unlike so many other projects this did not cause the total abandonment of these churches. Visionary spires require visionary architects. None of the churches in this book has been denied visionary architects, on the contrary many of them have had more visionary architects than they or their authorities knew what to do with. But in many cases, indeed all too many cases, visionary architects lacked the means to complete their schemes. Cologne and the two churches at Bristol show us two atypical reasons for optimism. Is it too much to hope that some time in the near future, some time in the distant future, churches such as Malines in Belgium and some of the other ignored and incomplete churches that we have considered, will finally be completed in the glory of their original designs?

148 Cologne Cathedral as it was at the end of
the Middle Ages; on the left is the east end,
with rudimentary walls of the transepts.
The nave, barely started, had houses built
upon it. On the right the bulk of the
unfinished south-west tower topped by the
crane that dominated views of the city.
From a painting by J. H. Hintze in Berlin.

149 Watercolour of 1840 showing Cologne Cathedral from the west, the south-west tower isolated from the incomplete walls of the nave.

151 By 1869, the north-west tower had reached the same height as its medieval colleague to the south. Already the extreme vertical emphasis of the design was apparent.

150 Vast changes were brought about at Cologne in the 1860s: by 1865, most of the nave had been built, and a start had been made on the west front.

152 Over 500 years after it was designed, the medieval façade of Cologne Cathedral was finally completed. It has been criticised for the heaviness of its ornamental details, such as the crockets which complete the spires, but the majesty of the spires reaching 500 feet high, is unarguable.

153 'Cologne Cathedral, as completed 1880, with reminiscences of its aspect at previous periods' published in *The Builder*.

154 Bristol Cathedral was unfortunate enough to be left without a nave at the Reformation: here it is portrayed on a roundel in the British Museum.

155 Bristol Cathedral completed in the nineteenth century to designs by G. E. Street. The nave continued the hall-church scheme of the fourteenth-century choir.

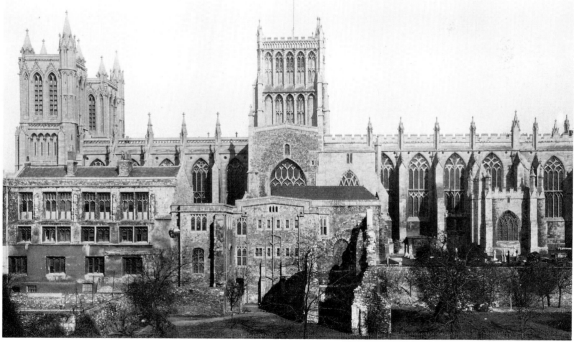

156 St. Mary Redcliffe, Bristol. The spire struck by lightning in the fifteenth century, was left truncated for five hundred years.

157 The damage belatedly put right. St. Mary Redcliffe with its spire restored to its medieval height.

Acknowledgements

The research for this volume has involved the writers' use of many archives and their helpful staff. In particular, all concerned with these endeavours are grateful to the following:
The staff of the British Museum, Cambridge University Library, Chester City Archives, Liverpool City Library, Sir John Soane's Museum, the Royal Institute of British Architects and the Victoria and Albert Museum. Of many kind individuals we thank Finch Allibone, Clare Best, G. D. Bye, Stephen Croad, Michael D. Lampen, Jill Lever, N.H. MacMichael, Godfrey New, Mrs E. Nixon, Roger Norris, Norma Potter, Jane Preger, Charles Quayle, Margaret Richardson, Sarah Sears, Sarah Shalgosky and Eileen Tweedy.

The publishers are grateful to the following for their gracious permission to reproduce material in this book.

Black and White Illustrations

The Warden and Fellows of All Souls College, Oxford *1, 59, 61, 67, 68;* The Dean and Chapter of Westminster *2;* The Dean and Chapter of Durham *3;* The Royal Commission on the Historical Monuments of England *4, 5, 88, 89, 90, 91, 101, 115, 122, 137, 138, 146, 154, 155, 156, 157;* Chester Archaeological Society and Chester City Record Office *6;* Liverpool City Libraries *7, 116, 117, 118, 119, 120, 121, 136;* The Board and Trustees of the Victoria and Albert Museum, London *8, 11, 13, 14, 15, 72, 73, 85, 86, 114, 135;* The Warden and Fellows of Worcester College, Oxford *9;* Biblioteca Ambrosiana, Milano *16;* Biblioteca Nazionale, Firenze *17;* The British Museum *18, 19, 20;* The British Architectural Library, RIBA, London *21, 22, 45, 46, 48, 49, 50, 80, 81, 82, 83, 84, 92, 93, 94, 96, 97, 98, 99, 100, 107, 108, 109, 110, 111, 112, 113, 132, 133, 141, 142, 143, 144, 145, 147, 148, 149, 150, 151, 152, 153;* The Syndics of Cambridge University Library *51, 52, 55, 56, 57, 70, 71, 74, 75, 76, 77, 78, 79, 95, 123, 124, 125, 126, 127, 128, 129, 130, 131;* Archivio della V. Fabbrica del Duomo, Milano *34, 35, 36, 37, 38, 39, 40, 41, 42, 43;* Graphischesammlung Albertina, Vienna *47;* The Trustees of the Chatsworth Settlement, Chatsworth *53, 54;* The National Portrait Gallery, London *58, 69, 139, 140;* Dean and Chapter of St. Paul's Cathedral, London *60, 62, 63, 64, 65, 66;* The Bodleian library, Oxford *80;* Grace Cathedral Archives, San Fransisco *102, 103;* Hunterian Art Gallery, University of Glasgow, Mackintosh Collection *134.*

Colour plates

The Dean and Chapter of Westminster *I;* The Vatican Library *II;* The British Architectural Library, RIBA, London *III, X, XI, XV, XVI, XVII, XVIII;* The Board and Trustees of the Victoria and Albert Museum *IV, V, VII, VIII, XII, XIII, XIV, XIX;* The Warden and Fellows of All Souls College, Oxford *VI;* Sir John Soane's Museum, London *IX;* Thorp Modelmakers Limited, London *XX.*

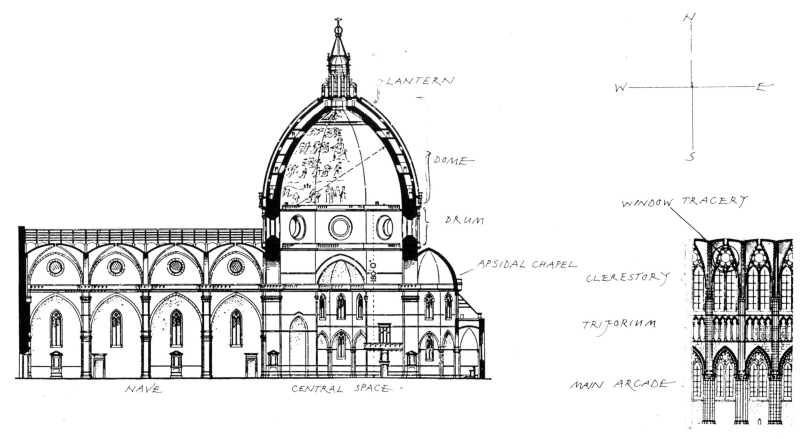

LANTERN

DOME

DRUM

APSIDAL CHAPEL

NAVE

CENTRAL SPACE

N

W — E

S

WINDOW TRACERY

CLERESTORY

TRIFORIUM

MAIN ARCADE

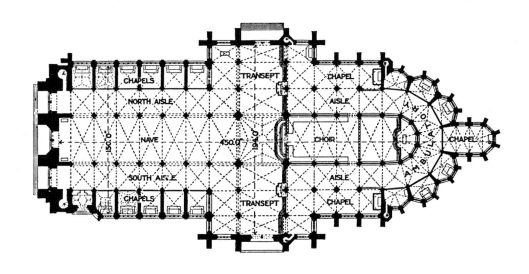

CHAPELS

TRANSEPT

CHAPEL

NORTH AISLE

AISLE

NAVE

CHOIR

AMBULATORY

CHAPEL

SOUTH AISLE

AISLE

CHAPELS

TRANSEPT

CHAPEL

Suggested Reading

The following architectural periodicals of the nineteenth and twentieth centuries have proved of the utmost importance for this book:

The Architects' Journal
The Architectural Review
The Builder
The Building News
The American Architect and Building News

Harper, R: *Victorian Architectural Competitions. An Index to British and Irish Architectural Competitions in The Builder 1843 – 1900*, London 1983, is a vital guide.

Selected short list of further titles

Academy Editions Architectural Monographs *John Soane*, London 1983
Arts Council, *Lutyens: The Work of the English Architect Sir Edwin Lutyens (1869 – 1944)*. Exhibition catalogue.

Blunt, A: *Artistic Theory in Italy, 1450 – 1600,* Oxford 1956.
Cole, D: *The Work of Sir Gilbert Scott*, London 1980.
Colvin, H: *The Biographical Dictionary of British Architects 1600 – 1840*, 2nd edition London 1978.
Crook, J M: *William Burges and the High Victorian Dream*, London 1981.
Downes, K: *The Architecture of Wren*, London 1982.
Frankl, P: *The Gothic*, Princeton 1962.
Gomme, A; Jenner, M; Little, B: *Bristol, An Architectural History*, London 1979.
Harris, J; Lever, J; Richardson, M: *Great Drawings from the Collection of the Royal Institute of British Architects*, London 1983.
Harris, J & Tait, A A: *Catalogue of the Drawings of Inigo Jones, John Webb and Isaac de Caus at Worcester College Oxford*, Oxford 1979.
Harvey, J: *Gothic England 1300 – 1550*, 2nd edition London 1948.
Harvey, J: *The Gothic World*, London 1950.
Harvey, J: *The Master Builders*, London 1971.
Irving, R G: *Indian Summer, Lutyens, Baker and Imperial Delhi*, New Haven 1981.
Murray, P: *Renaissance Architecture*, New York 1971.
Muthesius, S: *The High Victorian Movement in Architecture 1850 – 1870*, London 1972.
Norberg-Schulz, C: *Baroque Architecture*, New York 1971.
Ochsner, J K: *H H Richardson: Complete Architectural Works*, Massachusetts 1982.
Pevsner, N: *London, Volume One* (Buildings of England), 3rd edition revised by Bridget Cherry, Harmondsworth 1973.
Pommer, R: *Eighteenth-Century Architecture in Piedmont*, New York 1967.
Portoghesi, P: *Roma Barocca*, Cambridge Massachusetts 1971.
Portoghesi, P: *The Rome of Borromini*, New York 1968.
Quinney, A: *John Loughborough Pearson*, New Haven 1979.
Sitwell, S: *Southern Baroque Revisited*, London 1967.
Stroud, D: *Soane*, London 1984.
Summerson, J: *Architecture in Britain 1530 – 1830*, 7th edition Harmondsworth 1983.
Swaan, W: *Art and Architecture of the Late Middle Ages*, London 1977.
Thompson, P: *William Butterfield*, London 1971.
Withey, H F & Withey E R: *Biographical Dictionary of American Architects (Deceased)*, Los Angeles 1970.
Wittkower, R: *Art and Architecture in Italy 1600 – 1750*, Harmondsworth 1958.
Wittkower, R: *Gothic vs. Classic*, New York 1974.
Wittkower, R & Jaffé, J: *Baroque: The Jesuit Contribution*, New York 1972.
Wölfflin, H: *Renaissance and Baroque*, Ithaca 1966.

■ **A**achen (Aix-La-Chapelle) 128
Albany Cathedral 88-89, *93, 94, 95, 96*
Alberti, Leone Battista 48
Altenburg 77
American Architect and Building News, The 88, 90-91, 97-98
Amiens Cathedral 14, 91
Amati, Carlo 41
Angoulême 106
Antwerp Cathedral 12, 15
Architect's Journal, The 121
Austin and Paley 108-109, 116
■ **B**alcarres, Earl of 121
Barry, Sir Charles 75
Bassi, Martino 39
Beresford-Hope, A.J. 78
Bernini, Gianlorenzo 20, 25, 33, 41, 50, 57, 59
Beverley Minster 67
Birmingham, St. Chad's Cathedral 76
Blois, Château of 50
Boblinger, Matthaus 14
Bodley and Garner 104-106, 112
Bodley, G.F. 77, 80, 89-91, 108-109, 110, *102, 103*
Boisserée, Sulpice 129-130
Bologna 38
Bonaparte, Napoleon 41, 130
Borromeo, Carlo 23-24, 38-39
    Instructions for Ecclesiastical Buildings 38
Borromeo, Federico 40
Borromini, Francesco 48-49, *47, 48, 49*
Bramante, Donato 20-23, 25, 48, *26*
Brade, Daniel 41, *III*
Brentano, Giuseppe 41, *43*
Brewer, H.W. 12, 15, 104, *15, 114*
Brisbane Cathedral 79
Bristol, Cathedral 130-131, *154, 155*
    St. Mary Redcliffe 131, *156, 157*
Brodrick, C. *82*
Brooks, James 11, 104, 111
Brunelleschi, Filippo 22, 24
Brydon, John McKean 80, *87*
Builder, The 11, 75-77, 104-110, 122,
Builder's Journal, The 108-109
Building News, The 79-80
Burges, William 76-79, *84, 85, XII, XIII, XIV*
Burkhardt, Jacob 130
Butterfield, William 78
Buzzi, Carlo 40-41, *39*
    Lelio 39-40, *39*
■ **C**ambridge, King's College 68, 89, *79*
Cambridge Camden Society 75, 77
Campbell, Colen 67
    Vitruvius Britannicus 67, *74, 75*
Canterbury Cathedral 90, *101*
Caradosso 20, *18*

Carrère and Hastings 97, *104*
Cartaro, Mario 48
Casey, Edward 97
Castelli, Francesco 40-41
Castiglione, Sabba 21, 23
Chalon, M.R. 15
Chambers, Sir William 67, *72, 73, VIII*
Champneys, Basil 108
Charles II, King of England 7, 63
Charles Emmanuel II, Duke of Savoy 50
Chatsworth House 50
Chester Cathedral 10, 104, *5, 6*
Christian, Ewan 79
Church Building Act, The 68
Clutton, Henry 76
Cologne, Cathedral 78, 128-136 *148, 149, 150, 151,*
    152, 153
Competitions, Architectural 41, 76-77, 88, 97-99,
    104-110, 121-122.
Congdon, Henry M. 89, *98*
Constantinople, English Crimea Memorial Church
    76-77, *81* Sta. Sophia 22, 121
Cook, James H. 108
Corbetta, Antonio Maria 38-39
Cordini, Antonio *30*
Cork Cathedral 79
Corlette, H.C. 108, 110
Cotognola, Antonio Maria Vertermate 41, 45
Counter Reformation 23, 38
Country Life 121
Cram, Ralph Adams 99
Cram, Goodhue and Ferguson 89, *99*
Crombach, Hermann 128-129
■ **D**enver, Cathedral of St. John in the Wilderness 89-91,
    97, 98, 99, 100
Doane, William Croswell 88
Downey, Archbishop Richard 121
Drew, Sir Thomas 108
Dupérac, Etienne 25, *20*
Durham Cathedral 9, *3, 4*
■ **E**cclesiological Society, The 77-78
Ecclesiologist, The 75, 77
Edbrook, F.E. & Co. 89
Edinburgh, St. Mary's Cathedral 11, 79, *84*
Edward VII, King of England 110
Ely Cathedral 59, 105
Emerson, G.W. 104-107, *118-122*
Engleberg, Burkhard 14
Ensigen, Ulrich von 14
Erasmus 24
■ **F**arnese, Cardinal Alessandro 48
Ferratino, Bartolomeo 23
Ficino, Marsilio 21
Field and Medary 89-94

Fifty New Churches Act 68
Filarete, Antonio 17
    Tratti di Architettura 21
Florence, Cathedral 22, 24, 38, 50, 105
Fontana, Carlo 66
    Church of Sta. Maria Novella 48
Fontana, Domenico 25, 37
Foreman and Cameron *X*
Förster, Otto von 22
Francesca, Piero della 21
Francis Borgia, St. 48
Frederick Barbarossa 128
Freiburg Cathedral 14
■ **G**alliori, Guilio 41
Gandy, J.M. 68, *IX*
Gerona Cathedral 98
Gibberd, Sir Frederick 122
Gibbs, James 66-67, *69*
    Book of Architecture 66, *70, 71, 76, 77, 78*
Gibson, R.W. 88-89, 98, *105*
Giocondo, Fra 20-21, 23
Giorgio, Francesco di 21
Goethe, Johann Wolfgang von 129
    Von Deutsche Baukunst 129
Goodhue, B.G. 97
Gloucester Cathedral 89
Guarini, Guarino 48-49
    Architettura Civile 49-50, *51 52, 55-77*
■ **H**alsey Wood, William 97-99, *112, 113*
Hamburg, Church of St. Nicholas 77
Hare, Cecil Greewood 90
Hastings, Church of Our Lady Star of the Sea 108
Hawksmoor, Nicholas 8, 67-68, *2, 79*
Hay, James 104
Heins and La Farge 97, 99, *108, 109*
Henry VIII, King of England 130
Hoar Cross 89
Hobart, George P. 90-91
Hochstaden, Archibishop Konrad von 128
Hollar, Wenceslaus 15, *10, 15*
Hooke, Sir Robert 58
Hultz, Johan 14, *12*
Huss and Buck 97-98, *110-111*
Hussey, Christopher 121-122
■ **I**gnatius Loyola, St. 48
■ **J**esuits, Order of 48
Jones, Inigo 13, 57, 59, *9*
Juvarra, Filippo 41, 49-50, *53, 54*
■ **K**eldermans, Andries 15
    Antoon 15
Kent, Willaim *VII*
■ **L**emercier, Jacques 57
Leonardo da Vinci 21
    Sketchbooks 16

Lethaby, W.R. 110, *135, XIX*
Lightoler, T. 67
Ligorio, Piero 24
Lille Cathedral 11, 76-77, 78, *82, 83*
Lincoln Cathedral 14, 105
Lisbon, Sta. Maria della Providenza 49
Liverpool, Cathedral (Anglican) 11, 104-110, *7,*
   114-138, XV-XIX
   Cathedral (Roman Catholic) 120-122,*143-146, XX*
   Church of St. John, 104
   Church of St. Paul 67
   Church of St. Peter 104
   Lime Street Station 104
   St George's Hall 104-5
Llandaff Cathedral 122
Loches 106
Lombardo, Christophoro 38
London, Banqueting House, The 57
   Christchurch, Clapton 78
   Christchurch, Spitalfields 68
   Church of St. Bride, Fleet Street 58
   Church of St. Martin in the Fields 66, *70, 71*
   Church of St. George, Southwark 76
   Church of St. Marylebone 67, *72, 73, VIII*
   Church of St. Peter, Vauxhall 78
   Crystal Palace, The 78
   Great Fire 1666, 57
   Lincoln's Inn Fields 68
   Parliament, Houses of 75
   Queen's House, The 57
   St. Paul's Cathedral 7, 13, 22, 41, 57-59, 105, *1,*
   59-68, VI
   Southwark Cathedral 76, *80*
   Westminster Abbey 8, 90, 122, *2, 147, I*
   York House, Pall Mall 67
Louvain, City Hall 129
   Collegiate Church of St. Pierre 15
Lutyens, Sir Edwin 120-122, *140-147, XX*
■ Mackintosh, C.R. 110, *134*
Maderno, Carlo 20, 25, *22*
Madrid, Escorial 39
Malines (Mechlin), Cathedral 15, 131, *15*
Manetti 20-21
Mantegna 21
Mechlin, See Malines
Medd, Henry 121
Messina, Church of Sta. Annunciata 49
Metsis, J. 15
Michelangelo 20, 22-25, 38, *20, 27*
Milan, Cathedral 21, 38-41, *33-44, III*
   Church of Sta. Maria della Grazie 21
Models, Architectural 15, 23, 24, 25, 48, 58, 121, 122, *19*
Monferrato, Church of S. Filippo in Casale 50, *55*
Mons, Church of Ste. Waudru 15, *14*
Montorio, Tempietto of S. Pietro 21
Morgan, William 88

Morris, William 78
■ New Delhi Cathedral 120-121, *141, 142*
New York, Cathedral of St. John the Divine 11, 97-99,
   104-113
Nicholas of Bonaventure 38
Nicholson, C.A. 108-110, *126, XVI, XVII, XVIII*
Nicholson, Harold 120
Nizza, Church of S. Gaetano 50, *57*
■ Ochsner, Geoffrey Carl 88
Oratorians, Order of 49
Orsenigo, Simone da 38
Orvieto Cathedral 50
Oxford, All Souls College 67
■ Palladio, Andrea 67
   Quattro Libri dell'Architettura 57
Paris, Cathedral of Notre Dame 79
   Church of Ste. Anne-la-Royale 49-50, *51, 52*
   Church of the Sorbonne 57
Parler, Heinrich 38
   Michael 14, 128
Passeri, E.B. 49
Pearson, J.L. 78, 80, 131, *89-92*
Pellegrini, Pellegrino 38-41, *33*
Périgueux 106
Peruzzi, Baldassare 23, *28*
Peterborough Cathedral 78, 80, 107, *91, 92*
Petrarch 128
Pevsner, Sir Nikolaus 104
Philip II, King of Spain 39
Pite, Arthur Beresford *133*
Popes, Julius II 20, 21
   Leo X 23
   Martin V 38
   Nicholas V 20
   Paul II 23
   Pius IV 38
   Urban VIII 49
Porta, Giacomo della 25, 48, *46*
Portoghesi 22
Potter and Robertson 97-98, *106, 107*
Pozzi, Andrea 67
Pratt, Sir Roger 58
Pugin, A.W. N. 75-78, 80
   An Apology for the Revival of Christian Architecture
   in England 75
   True Principles of Pointed or Christian Architecture,
   The 75, 88, 130
Pugin and Pugin 41
Pullan, R.B. 77, 80, *83-86*
■ *Quarterly Review, The* 68
■ Raphael 23, *29*
Reilly, C.H. 121-122
Reilly and Peach 108, 110, *130, 131*
Rheims Cathedral 14
Renwick, Aspinall and Russell 97
Ricchino, Francesco 39, 40, 44

Richardson, H.H. 88, 89, 91, *95*
Rickman, Thomas 75
Rome, Church of S. Carlo alle Quatro Fontane 49
   Church of S. Ivo della Sapienza 49, *50*
   Church of Sta. Maria Valicella 49
   Church of Sta. Susanna 39
   Gesù 48, *45, 46*
   Oratorio of S. Filippo Neri 48, 49, *47, 48, 49*
   St. Peter's Cathedral 20-25, 38, 48, 50, 106, 121-122,
   128, *18-32 II*
   Vatican 22, 25
   Via della Conciliazone 25
Ross, Alexander 79
Rossellino, Bernardo 20, 21
Ruskin, John 78
   The Seven Lamps of Architecture 78
   The Stones of Venice 78
Rughesi, Fausto 37, 49, *32*
■ St. Aubyn, James Piers 80
Salisbury Cathedral 9, 59, *XI*
Sancroft, Dean of St. Paul's 57
Sandrart, Joachim von 129
San Francisco, Grace Cathedral 90-91, *102, 103*
Sangallo, Giuliano da 20-25, 48, *19, 24, 30*
Schlegel, Friedrich von 129
Scott, Adrian Gilbert 122
   Sir George Gilbert 75, 77, 79, 80, *6*
   Recollections 75
   Sir Giles Gilbert 108-110, *123-124, 139*
   J. Oldrid 108, *125, XV*
Seregni, Vincenzo 38
Serlio, Sebastiano 23
   L'Architettura 23
Sforza, Lodovico 21
Sforzinda 21, *17*
Shaw, Richard Norman 108
Shrewsbury, Church of St. Chad 67
Siena Cathedral 38, 50
Skidmore, F.A. 79
Skipworth, A.H. 108, *132*
Slater, William 77-78
Soane, Sir John 68
Society for the Protection of Ancient Buildings, The 78
Spada, Virgilio 49
Stark, Malcolm 108, 109, *128*
Sterner, Frederick J. 90
Stornacolo, Gabriele 38
Strasbourg Cathedral 14-15, 128-129, *10-12*
Street, George Edmund 77-79, 98, 130, *81, 155*
   Brick and Marble in the Middle Ages 78
Stuart, George 67
Summerson, Sir John 57, 59, *67*
■ Tacitus 129
Tapper, W.J. 108-109, *129*
Togmi, Aristide de 41
Tracy and Swartwout 89, *97*

Trent, Council of 24, 38
Truro Cathedral 11, 79-80, *85-90, XII, XIII, XIV*
Turin, SS. Sindoni and Lorenzo 49, 50
    Superga 49
■ Ulm Minster 14-15, *13*
    Urbino 21
■ Vasari 21, 23-24, 39, 48, 129
    Vaughan, Henry 99
    Vercelli, Church of S. Andrea 77
    Vicenza, Church of S. Filippo 50
        Church of S. Gaetano 50, *56*

    Vienna Cathedral 14-15
    Vignola, Giacomo Barozzi da 39, 48, 51
    Vitruvius Britannicus – see Campbell, Colen
    Vittone, Bernardo 50, *42*
        Istruzzioni Elementari 49
■ Walley, F. 108
    Washington D.C., National Cathedral 99
    Webb, John 13, *9*
    Wells Cathedral 14, 91
    Willemstad, Fortress of 15
    Willson, Thomas 130

    Wittkower, Rudolf 38, 41
    Wren, Sir Christopher 7, 13, 22, 41, 57-59, 104-106,
        1, 58-68, VI
        Parentalia 58
    Wyatt, James 9, *3*
■ York Minster 14, 58, 106
■ Zurich Cathedral 78

9-29-91